The Taste of Essex

Ron Mullenger was born in London where he still lives. After spending his early years in the theatre, both on and off stage, he took up a career in business. He has been writing all his life but it wasn't until he retired that he turned professional.

Ron Mullenger

The Taste of Essex

AUSTIN MACAULEY
PUBLISHERS LTD.

I cannot make the disclaimer popular with writers of fiction who declare
that the persons coming to life in their narratives are entirely imaginary
and bear no intended resemblance to any person living or dead. Some of
my characters were real, others were... not quite, and a few, mainly the
unpleasant ones, are made up from whole cloth or patches from the same.

A CIP catalogue record for this title is available from the British Library.

ISBN 9781849632973

www.austinmacauley.com

First Published (2013)
Austin Macauley Publishers Ltd.
25 Canada Square
Canary Wharf
London
E14 5LB

Printed & Bound in Great Britain

Acknowledgements

My thanks to:-

Lorna Barclay for reading the manuscript.
Mr Stephen Scott – for allowing me to stay in his house in Chelmsford during the research period.

Also thanks to the following people for the use of recipes included in this book:

Mr Thorogood of S. Thorogood & Sons
Sarah Green of Sarah Green Organics
Mrs Partridge of Gate Farm
Stephen Pini, Executive Chef, Fishmongers Company
The late Molly Kelly of Kelly's Turkeys
J. Salmon Ltd. Sevenoaks, Kent
Mrs Shirley Trollope of Clay Barn
Matthew Rooney of Gourmet Mushrooms
Julie at Great Garnets
W H Marriage & Sons/Linda Collister
Calcott Hall Farm

1

Avoid the centre of London and the congestion charge and roar around the M25 to enter Essex via the Dartford Tunnel under the river. In these modern days of superstores and shopping malls, the first place of any interest you come to in the county is the Lakeside shopping complex in West Thurrock, which rivals Bluewater on the other side of the river. Here you will find hundreds of shops all waiting to relieve you of your money. All the big names are there, including Boots, Currys, Marks & Spencer, Miss Selfridge and Moss Bros, to name but a few. Also there are plenty of fast food outlets waiting to tempt you. In fact, if you can't find what you want in Lakeside Shopping Centre, you are very hard to please indeed. To get there and are approaching clockwise, take exit 30 off the M25, or if from the anti-clockwise direction, exit at junction 31, they will both lead you straight into the enormous car park, but do make sure you make a note of where you left your car!

After your shopping experience, provided you haven't spent all your money or bent your credit card to its limit, head into Grays Beach Riverside Park on New Road, Grays for a well earned rest. It also sounds like an exciting day out for the kids. There is a massive sand play area, you can buy buckets and spades and the kids can build sand castles. If this isn't enough, there's a bouncy castle, or if that's not good enough, they could try Britain's biggest play galleon and be Johnny Depp for a while. The café sells a variety of hot and cold refreshments, so you need not go hungry. You can even organise your child's birthday party there, when they could take a whole gang of their friends with them. You'll need a people carrier though, but with my lot, a char-a-banc would be more appropriate. For more information, ring 01275 386759.

A few miles further on from Grays is Tilbury from where, in the past, great ocean liners left for countries far away. Names like Peninsular and Oriental and Union Castle, whose ships took weeks to get you to New Zealand and South Africa. It is believed that it was on these grand steamers that the term 'posh' originated standing for port out and starboard home. Now somewhat sadly, the great liners of P & O do not sail out of Tilbury any longer, but they will still transport you across the channel and the docks at Tilbury only handle a very few cruise ships; most traffic now is cargo.

Tilbury is also the place where a fort dips its feet into the river. This is the spot where Queen Elizabeth I made her famous speech whilst awaiting the Spanish Armada. If she stood here now, she would be able to see the magnificent bridge, named after her namesake, Queen Elizabeth II. However, the old queen would not recognise anything, even the old fort built by her father had to make way for a better 17th century model. Tilbury Fort has been a symbol of the defence of London for over 400 years. It took the Second World War to inflict lasting damage on it; the army barracks were destroyed. However, although the cannons are still there, pointing out across the river, they are now silent, silent forever we hope. Tilbury Fort makes an interesting visit. Even if you are not a historian, you can get a lot out of a place that has been so important to this country's defence for so long and, standing there, you can really see why.

Another very interesting place to visit in this neck of the woods is the Walton Hall Museum of Memorabilia. Come off the A1013 just before Stanford Le Hope and make for Mucking and between this little hamlet and Linford is the Walton Hall Museum. Housed in a restored 17th century Essex barn, the displays include old farming implements, artefacts from both world wars, childrens' toys in a Victorian nursery, old radios and many, many more objects of yesteryear. It was the old radios that made me feel my age, as some of them I remember listening to. Outside the barn you will find old farm machinery, vintage tractors, road rollers and a Blacksmith's display. They even have an old Romany caravan, beautifully restored and resplendent in brilliant colours

The museum is only open Thursday to Sunday between April and November, 10am to 5pm. If you are dragging a caravan behind your car, there's a caravan site right there for you. Oh and by the way, if you are into the paranormal, the museum holds creepy investigations in the 17th century barn. Rather you than me!

This most southern area of Essex abounds with country parks. Names like Westley Heights, One Tree Hill, Hadleigh Castle but perhaps the best known is the Wat Tyler Country Park. It is situated at the head of Holehaven Creek near the village of Fobbing. I couldn't help wondering, as I entered the park, what its connection was with Mr Wat Tyler. This gentleman became the leader of the peasants' revolt in the 14th century but he had absolutely nothing to do with Fobbing. He was from across the river in Kent but Fobbing was where the revolt actually started. King Richard II had imposed a poll tax on everyone to pay for his war in France. The villagers of Fobbing didn't like it, so they revolted. I remember Margaret Thatcher had a similar problem with her poll tax! However, Wat Tyler was finally executed but his name lives on in the country park.

The Wat Tyler Centre explores the park's history and its future as a public open space and natural wildlife habitat. It also tells of the time in the 19th century when the area was an explosives factory. One wonders whether the munitions that helped win the battles of Trafalgar and Waterloo were made here. The site now has a nature trail and a sculpture walk where you will find some very interesting and unusual pieces of sculpture displayed along the way. Of particular interest to me was the Village Green. Here they have erected some historic Essex cottages. They removed them from their original sites and transported them brick by brick to the park. They make a pretty sight.

If you should decide to get married, you can do so in the Wat Tyler Centre in the park and if you should die, your family can hold a wake there also to celebrate your life. Now there's a thought.

A short distance from Wat Tyler, is a small family business called Home Fayre, tucked away in one unit of a small industrial complex in Basildon. They make cakes of many different varieties including banana cake, which I particularly liked. However, it was no surprise that carrot cake was their most popular. I have never really liked carrot cake; carrots for me are part of my meat and two veg, not as part of my afternoon tea! One of the company's proud boasts is their Impossible Cake. This contains no eggs, sugar, fat or milk, making it ideal for vegans, diabetics and dairy allergy sufferers. I was not given the opportunity of sampling it, so cannot say if it had any flavour at all but from what I could tell of Mark Whetton, the owner, I'm sure it does. They sell mainly to the wholesale trade, but they do appear at various farmers' markets throughout Essex. They have even done a car boot sale in Dunton. They sell regularly in the Pitsea markets. From small beginnings, they have now increased their production to between 6 and 7 hundred cakes a week. They are all handmade under strict hygiene conditions.

Mark started the business as a hobby 22 years ago and seems just as keen on the business now as he was then. He's a true Essex boy, liberally adorned with gold bracelets and rings, has a very pleasant, friendly attitude and was very welcoming.

Whilst they sometimes make savouries, they major on their cream cakes. The lead time is about 2 days. They will make different cakes to special order and they accept any order, large or small. They have made large cakes for special occasions, but this really is not their business.

On entering this small unit, I was immediately assailed with the smell of baking. It was a very pleasant introduction to the company of only three people, one of whom was Mark's sister. Although the unit is small, they seem to have managed to squeeze a quart into a pint pot. Immediately inside the front door, they wrap and pack and alongside are storage shelves holding hundreds of mouth-watering cakes awaiting delivery, which they do themselves in their own van. Deeper inside the room is where they make their cakes, using giant mixers, and beyond this is the single oven, which to my unpractised eye, looked ridiculously small for such a volume of production. At the far back of the room is a very tiny office, which Mark says is big enough for him as he spends very little time in it. He spends most of the time making his cakes.

All in all a very pleasant company producing an excellent product. I would say it was typical of the spirit, tenacity, enthusiasm and excellence that I have found all over Essex.

If you didn't like the Wat Tyler Country Park, there's another one you could visit in the area. Turn off the A13 at Hadleigh and follow the tourist signs to Hadleigh Country Park. It is named after the ruined fortress, Hadleigh Castle which was built in the 13th century. The ruins of the two remaining towers are set on a high ridge overlooking the park. They command wonderful views of the Thames Estuary, Canvey Island, the Kent coast, the Dartford Bridge and Canary Wharf.

There are many things to do and see in the park, which is particularly famous for its butterflies, birds of prey and practically every songbird in England. The park is laid out with wonderful walks, lasting anything from 30 minutes to an hour and a half but be careful where you walk, there are adders about.

Further downstream, where the river becomes sea, you will arrive at the one time fishing village of Old Leigh, now called Leigh-on-Sea, a suburb of Southend-on-Sea, although the old residents of Leigh would hate me for saying so. All these little towns have added on-sea to their names to distinguish them from the river. They are seaside not riverside. Little is left of Old Leigh but the High Street does retain a little of its old world charm. It is narrow, bordered by wooden clapboard cottages and a row of stalls known as the Cockle Sheds. At the end of the street is the 16th century listed building known as the Crooked Billet, the local pub.

The Cockle Sheds do, as the name suggests, sell cockles. From the 22nd June until November, early every morning the cockle boats come in to unload their catch on the beach behind the sheds. Most only sell wholesale but one, Estuary Fish Merchants at Cockle Shed Number eight, will sell you some, as will the Leigh Fishermans Co-operative. This is a must. Housed in what used to be a boat builders shed, it has the best display of fresh fish that I have ever seen outside Boulogne. Every kind of fish that swims in Essex waters, and some that don't, is on display. Believe me you will find every kind of creature that is ever pulled out of our sea waiting to delight you. This of course includes the cockles which, from sea to shop is only yards and you can't get them fresher than that. Incidentally, cockles actually come in shells, not as I thought, in vinegar. When I was there I bought some scallops and paid a lot less for them than I would have in London, and they came in their shells, which is rare now in London. The shop was very busy and from what I could see, has only one salesman, so you must expect to wait in a queue, but it will be well worth the wait.

There are many ways of serving cockles but the way I like is to put unopened cockles in cold water, bring to the boil and take them out. Remove them from their shells, make a batter which should include a little beer. Coat the cockles well and deep fry in hot fat for a few minutes only. Forget the vinegar!

Another local speciality, much beloved of Londoners, is jellied eels. In the Co-operative you will find glistening bowls of them waiting to be consumed. In the summer, people come from the east end in droves to holiday beside the sea. They make short work of them, washed down with several pints of beer from the local pub, The Crooked Billet.

Leigh-on-Sea appears to be a quiet place out of the holiday season, but looks can be deceiving. All around you is the bric-a-brac of fishing and boat building, repairing nets, painting boats, getting ready for the season. But from June to November the beach is a hive of early morning activity and the pub gets a roaring trade. The view from the beach across the estuary is to the misty Kent coast and towards the east, is the outline of the world's longest pier.

While I was wandering around Leigh, I bumped into Bryn Taylor. Bryn is an ex-insurance broker who got fed up with the rat-race in the city and, four years ago, set up his company which he called 'The Chilli Chutney Man'. He makes an astounding range of everything chilli. Some products sound dangerous like Nitronaga chilli sauce, which, he says will blow your mind. His range goes from mind blowing, through stupid hot, hot and fairly hot. He pickles shallots, with chilli of course, and a ginger chilli marinade, which sounds interesting. His chutneys include Spicy Fig, Bolivian Chilli Jam, Boozy Chutney and many, many more. Some of his chutneys are sugar free too.

Now to order you can telephone him on 01702 470502 or his mobile 07929 918408, or by e-mail chillichutneyman@tiscali.co.uk If you are in his area, he will deliver or if not, post to you. Payment is by cheque on delivery. However I would recommend that you try before you buy, in which case, visit one of the following farmers' markets. Leigh-on-Sea during June to November, Maldon the last Sunday in the month, Danbury the first Saturday in the month or at the Hyde Hall Market. He also attends what he calls 'Ladies Pampering Parties'. If nothing else, I'm sure he's the man to heat the ladies up!

If you happen to be down Southend way in the run up to Christmas, you may well be wanting a Christmas tree. At this time of the year there are more trees in florists, garden centres, farmers' markets and supermarkets than you can shake a stick at. Even my local convenience store has a pavement full of them. I'm quite sure they can't sell them all. However, if you find yourself in the Rochford area, bowl along to Hawkwell, find Rectory Road and there you will find Essex's own Christmas Tree Farm. They have thousands of the things in various stages of growth. You can buy a tree in a pot, small enough to sit on a window sill or one up to twenty feet tall. But don't get carried away, for unless you live in a marbled hall, a 20ft tree would push your ceiling out.

The farm is only open during December, from 9am to 6pm, which is reasonable because not many people want a Christmas tree in June. The farm will not only cut the tree fresh for you, they will also sell you a stand to put it in and decorations to put on it. They claim that their trees do not lose their needles, but I have never put that to the test. Also while you're there, you might as well pick up a holly wreath as well.

Southend seems to be a shadow of its former self. It used to be a place where London families came for their holiday. Where they could spend the day in the famous Kursaal, enjoying the rides, playing the machines and generally having fun. Nowadays the Kursaal has a function suite where you can get married, a casino where you can go broke and a Tesco superstore. In those days the boys could enjoy their beer and jellied eels but today it would seem that the beer tastes better in Benidorm and Ibiza. There, they may not get jellied eels, but they can get fish and chips. About the only thing that remains the same in Southend is the pier. You can still take a stroll or ride the mile by train to the pier head.

On your way to Hawkwell you will pass Southend airport. Some years ago, you could fly to many European destinations from there; you could even fly your car to Ostend. I remember putting my car on a plane at Southend bound for Belgium. It was quite exciting knowing that your car was under your seat in the cargo hold in a plane just a few feet above the waves. You can't do that anymore. All you can now do is fly to Jersey, to Galway and Waterford. So if you are after some Waterford glass bargains, Southend Airport is the place to start from.

2

If you happen to be driving north on the A130, turn off at the junction with A132 and head for Battlesbridge. Sited a little way down Woodham Road you will find Allens Farm Shop. This is typical of farm shops throughout the whole of Essex, crammed full of the very best of local produce. A charming young lady called Kay introduced me to a number of products that I had never seen before. One was Pombears crisps. These are potato crisps made in the shape of teddy bears. Now they have to be a hit with the kids. They are only one of some very unusual merchandise Kay offers. For your dog she has pigs' ears for Fido to gnaw on for hours. Better for him than a chocky drop.

All their fruit and vegetables are grown on the farm. As soon as they come out of the ground, within minutes they are on sale in the shop. Can't get fresher than that. I saw that the sprouts on sale were still attached to their stems. Kay told me that they keep much fresher like that. In fact, in the winter, sometimes the snow is still clinging to the sprouts in the shop. There are many other Essex products on display including Wilkins jam, local honey and bacon. Kay also sells a wide range of potatoes, grown locally by G R French whose premises are right next door. If you find yourself in the area, it would be well worth a stop, but take plenty of bags with you.

Many people, not only children, don't like Brussels Sprouts. Memories of over-boiled sprouts tasting disgusting. The real secret is not to boil them too long. What I do is, place them into cold water (I know this is supposed to be wrong, but never mind), bring them to the boil, turn the gas off and leave them in the water. Then I chop up some streaky bacon and dry fry it to leach out as much fat as possible. It is better to use really good bacon for this because the supermarket stuff merely leaches out water. If you don't get enough fat, add a teaspoon of vegetable oil. Cut off slivers of ginger root, add to the bacon, then throw in the sprouts and cook for a few minutes over medium heat making sure that they are completely coated. Of course it is better to use sprouts from the stem. I tried this recipe out recently on a friend who hated Brussels. She ate the lot!

I have already mentioned that the potato merchants, G R French are right next door to Allens, but don't go there for they do not sell retail. However, next time you enjoy a plate of fish and chips in almost any fish shop in Essex, you can bet your life that the potatoes came from G R French.

There are literally hundreds of ways to cook potatoes but what I'm interested in is what to do with leftover mash. If you've got any cold meat, doesn't matter what it is, mince it up, mix with the mash, add a beaten egg, form into rounds and fry them up. You can also do this with any leftover vegetables; chop them up for a bubble and squeak. Or you can be a bit more adventurous, using a potato peeler, sliver off some raw carrot and mix in, then fry.

Carry on the A132 to South Woodham Ferrers, here you will find one of Essex's small breweries, Crouch Vale Brewery on Haltwhistle Road. The brewery is named after the river which splashes by on its way to Burnham and claims to be the oldest, continuously working brewery in Essex. Even so it is a modern gem. Its products are all cask ales, the only acceptable beer drunk by real ale officianales. They have five regular ales, the mildest at 3.5 ABV called Essex Boys, seems to me to be a bit of a misnomer. In increasing strengths are Blackwater Mile, Crouch Best, Brewers Gold, which is their award winning beer, and Amarillo – an ale that could bite you at 5.0ABV. They also produce seasonal beers like Golden Duck and Santas Revenge, which at 5.0ABV, speaks for itself.

They seem to be an enterprising company in that they swap their beers with other independent brewers. For instance, if a Scottish brewer wants to sell his beer in East Anglia, Crouch Vale will stock it in return for the Scottish brewer selling theirs. Sounds like a good arrangement to me.

Another unusual aspect to their business is that they scour the hedgerows along the lanes, highways and byways of Essex for wild hops. I didn't know that hops grow wild in Essex, but it seems we have more wild hops than any other county. They then use these very local hops to brew their very local beer. I asked the general manager ,Olly Graham, how they collected these hops. Apparently several employees go out with secateurs searching. I can see Olly himself going out at the dead of night armed with a torch and secateurs.

Naturally you will want to know where you can buy this nectar. Marks and Spencer and Tesco stock it, but only in Essex. Apart from that, the Fat Cat pub in Colchester stocks it, as does Crouch Vale's own pub, The Queens Head in Chelmsford. Also you can turn up at the brewery and, provided you buy enough, you can get it at the gate.

Most people will have heard the expression 'a p*** up in a brewery', well here you can. As long as you have a minimum of fifteen people in a group, for a tenner a head, you can have a tour of the brewery starting at 7pm week nights and ending up at the Queens Head, Chelmsford for a light supper, all included. Might be a good way to celebrate a birthday.

Lying neatly alongside the River Crouch at South Wodham Ferrers you will find the Marsh Farm Country Park. Owned by Essex County Council, this country park claims to be a working farm. However, I saw little evidence of farming whilst I was there; the animals all appear to be merely for looking at. If you happen to be interested in wildlife, Marsh Farm Park is well worth a visit for a day out. There are plenty of things for kids to do. For instance, during the school holidays there is a Treasure Hunt. You have to find the clues, which are scattered around the park. Also you can have tractor rides or pony rides. You can participate in some pony grooming, have your face painted and even handle some of the pet animals. However, after touching animals please make sure you all wash your hands, or use the cleansing gel provided. If you wish to feed the animals, you must buy the proper feed from the shop.

The farm is open daily from 13th February to 29th October and in November and December, weekends only. When I was there the entrance fee was £7.50 for an adult and £4.50 for a child. But don't bank on it being the same now. Sorry, you can't take your dog with you. The farm has an animal adoption scheme where for £35 you can adopt a pet of your choice for one year. I'm not too sure what this entails, but you could find out by dialling 01245 321552. The farm is open for hire for birthday parties and, around Halloween they hold a Pumpkin Week, which could be fun. At Christmas, old Santa Claus himself visits the farm.

Also in South Woodham Ferrers is the Tropical Wings Zoo in Wickford Road.

Tropical Wings Zoo is justly famous for two things. First it has the world's largest butterfly house. Inside there are hundreds of free flying butterflies. Make sure they don't settle in your hair. Secondly they are famous for the Mangalitzas. These creatures originated in Hungary and Austria and are very rarely seen in England. They are pigs that have a woolly coat, just like a sheep. Curious animals, they are fun to stroke, if they'll let you. One question I had, do they have to be sheared? Perhaps you can find out for me. Tropical Wings Zoo is open every day in the winter from 10am to 4.30pm and in the summer, 9.30am to 5.30pm.

The Royal Horticultural Society Garden at Hyde Hall, Rettenden is surely worth a day out. When I last went there it appeared as if some great giant had picked it up and turned it round 180 degrees and put it down again. When I approached what I believed to be the main entrance, I found that it was no longer. The gate was locked and a notice told me that it was for deliveries only. It gave me no information as to where the entrance now was, but I carried on regardless. I drove round the estate to the other side and, sure enough found a gate. I nearly missed it though because the entrance sign had its back to me. It only wanted to tell people approaching from the other direction, where it was.

On the drive up to the car park it was clear that great changes had taken place and in fact were still ongoing. The car park has been enlarged but even so, at Easter, it was almost full. Once through the shop, tickets purchased, I was confronted with several acres of barren earth. In the due course of time this area will obviously be planted up. I'm sure now it will be a picture of beauty, as is the rest of the garden. Hyde Hall has many specimen plants and even wildlife to enjoy. Easter is perhaps not the best time to visit the garden, in spite of the crocuses and daffodils because a lot of the most valuable plants were still wearing their winter overcoats.

Even during a make-over and my visit being early in the year, I really did enjoy the place and I know that in summer, it is very beautiful. Enjoy the walks and listen to the birds as well as getting a lot of gardening information from the experts.

Carry on the B1012 toward Burnham-on-Crouch and turn right when you see the sign to Fambridge. If I remember rightly it indicates to The Marina. Anyway, carry on this Ferry Lane and after a few hundred yards you will arrive at Whitehouse Farm. Jack Friedlein, the owner, describes himself as an Animal Control & Capture Specialist. What this means is that he is available to humanely kill any escaped, injured or dangerous animal and is often called upon to do so. So if you happen to have lost your wild cat, he's your man.

His other business is rearing and producing venison. Up to about eighteen years ago he was a dairy farmer but he changed and started to breed deer. He now has about 260 of which, at any one time, might include up to 100 breeding hinds. They are born, reared and slaughtered right here on the farm. The herd are mostly Fallow and Red Deer and it produces about 90/95 calves in the season. Jack mostly supplies butchers shops, hotels, restaurants and local farmers' markets with joints, steaks, sausages, mince and casserole meat. He does not deliver but if you order in advance on 01621 740421, you can collect from the farm gate.

Venison stew is one of my favourite meals. What I do is this: Cut the meat into chunks, seal it on all sides in hot fat and put into a casserole. Add any vegetables of your choice – onions and carrots are my favourite. Add a bay leaf, rosemary and/or thyme and garlic, chopped. Mix some red wine with olive oil and pour over the meat and leave overnight. When ready to cook, put some chunks of dark chocolate into the casserole and mix well. Season with salt and black pepper and place in a medium oven and cook until the meat is very tender.

While I was in North Fambridge I noticed a white van parked on the side of the road, which had painted on its side, 'Essex Hog Roasts'. This was too good to miss, so I decided to investigate. Essex Hog Roasts is a catering company supplying whole pigs, suckling pigs, lamb and beef split roasts. They can even supply you with a complete barbeque and giant vegetarian paellas. They cater mainly for weddings, corporate events and private parties. So if you have an anniversary coming up and wish to throw a party, Hog Roasts will do everything for you. They will even supply crockery, cutlery and napkins. Give them a call on 01621 826793 and they will be happy to give you a quote.

Alternatively, if you are not intending to splash out on a party, you could catch Essex Hog Roasts at the Weald Show and the Epping Forest Festival and sample their wares.

One day I was recommended to contact Beatbush Organic Farm in Latchingdon but, try as I might I just couldn't find it. I very soon gave up and carried on my way. Some time later I met a man who told me he knew the owner of Beatbush Farm very well and knew exactly where it was. He drew me a map in my notebook, which I followed and found the place. In fact Beatbush is the name of the company, the farm is Brookhall Farm; no wonder I couldn't find it.

Latchingdon is a village on the road from Maldon to Burnham, but when you get to the village, do not follow the main road, but where it turns sharp right, keep straight on. This is Steeple Road which leads to a village deep in the Dengie peninsular called Steeple, where else? Brookhall Farm is on the right side of the road, a couple of miles further on from the village. In fact, this is academic for you have no need to visit because they do not sell at the farm gate.

When I got to the farm there appeared to be no one around. I did have the telephone number, so I called. The owner answered - she was in Norfolk. They have another farm in Methwold. She told me that Beatbush Organic Farm is a family-run outfit producing organic beef, lamb, geese and turkeys. They do not sell retail but you can get their produce from The Food Company in Marks Tey or Lathcoats in Galleywood. They also appear at the Maldon Farmers' Market on the first Tuesday of every month, except January. Make a date in your diary, try some and you'll be amazed at how much better their meat tastes.

If you do decide to try organic beef, I believe one of the best ways to eat it is cold but you need the best quality beef for this and Beatbush produce it. There was an old fashioned recipe for spiced beef that my grandmother used to do. So why not spice a piece of organic beef up a bit. You can use any cut of beef, rump, silverside, but my grandmother used brisket. This is what you do.

Into about a quarter of a pint of malt vinegar put about four tablespoons of soft brown sugar, about half a teaspoon of pepper; I use white because it looks better, three or four cups of sea salt and about half a teaspoon of mixed spice. Mix it well and marinate the beef in it. Make sure the beef is completely covered and keep it in the fridge for up to a week, turning is over occasionally.

After the week, take the meat out, rinse it well in cold water. Put it in a flameproof casserole dish together with any vegetables you fancy, carrots, turnips, parsnips or onions.

Cover with cold water, bring it to the boil and simmer slowly for up to five hours, or until the meat is very tender. When done, take it out and place on a platter, put a dinner plate on top and put a heavy weight on top of the plate. Leave in the fridge overnight. Then, slice and enjoy.

At the nearby village of Althorne is Highfield Farm the home of Althorne Beef. Again it is not easy to find and I had to ask directions. In the centre of the village you will see the parish hall. Exactly opposite you will see a narrow lane. Highfield Farm is where the lane ends. There is no name or sign but don't be deterred, drive on past a livery stables and at the end of the lane – Highfield Farm.

I knocked on the front door of a somewhat modern looking farmhouse and was greeted by Mrs White. She runs a small unit of only thirty-four shorthorn cattle which produces the most wonderful meat. If you telephone 01621 741845 in advance, you can buy joints from 2/3 lb up to 8/9 lb at the farm gate. Or you can of course visit the local farmers' markets where Althorne beef is much in demand by those who know a good thing when they see it.

An idea for eating beef is my own version of Angels on Horseback, which I call Beef Angels. Take a nice piece of Althorne Beef topside and slice it as thin as you can. If you can get your hands on a rotary slicer, so much the better but do keep your hands away from the blade. You want the slices to be a thin as possible to make them easier to roll. Now lay a strip of streaky bacon on each beef slice; you can add a little chopped onion on each slice, although this is not necessary. Roll them up and fix with a wooden toothpick or cocktail stick. Brown them in a little olive oil and then remove them from the pan. Pour in about three-quarters of a pint of beef stock, made from a stock cube, scrape the bottom of the pan to loosen any bits. Now add chopped vegetables of your choice and a bouquet garni. Bring to the boil and then replace the beef. Simmer gently for about an hour or until tender. Remove the Angels from the pan, keep warm while you boil the vegetables in the stock until it has reduced a little, then pour it over the Angels.

As I drove from Althorne towards Burnham, I passed a somewhat ordinary looking farm shop, Wrekin Farm Products. I stopped and went in. Inside I found it to be a treasure trove of Essex products. It was divided into two separate areas, one for fresh meat and the other for more delicatessen type products. Nearly everything in the shop comes from Essex producers and, while I was there, they seemed to be doing a roaring trade, especially as they seem to be miles from anywhere. On the map it says they are at a place called Ostend, but don't be fooled, you don't have to cross the channel. So, if you happen to be in the area, don't judge a farm shop by its front, call in.

3

On the road to Burnham on Crouch I noticed a sign pointing to a place called Creeksea. Having never heard of it, I took the road and found myself at Creeksea Place. This 16th century mansion is known as the hidden jewel of Essex. It was tucked away down a small, badly kept, leafy lane and was quite difficult to find. However, keep your eyes open until you see a sign directing you to Creeksea Caravan Park. Carry on, ignore Creeksea Hall – a private house – until you come to a rather dilapidated gateway and through it you will discover this Elizabethan jewel.

Creeksea Place is reputed to have been the home of Anne Boleyn and it has been said that her ghost can sometimes be seen in and around the house. I wonder if she is complete with her head or not. The house has another macabre connection with death. Lord Mildmay, Keeper of the Crown Jewels for King Charles 1st, became the owner of Creeksea Place and he became one of the signatories to the death warrant of the king.

But happier times prevail today, for although it is not lived in, it is available for hire for weddings, christenings and wakes. You can hire the place for a party for up to 150 guests but they tell me 120 is a more convenient number. So if you would like to get married in a fairytale environment, Creeksea is the place for you.

If you approach Burnham-on-Crouch on the B1010, turn left when you reach Southminster Road, B1021 and take the first turning on your right. This is Marsh Road; carry on for a few hundred yards and you will come to one of Essex's worst kept secrets. The Secret Butchers Shop. Now they mainly sell wholesale, but in a chilled cabinet they do have a limited selection of beef, pork and lamb for retail sale.

One of their most famous products is the Burnham Banger. I was introduced to the young butcher who is in charge of sausage production and he showed me how he did it. Following this, I had to buy some, naturally. I took them home and found how truly delicious they were.

The Burnham Banger is so good, it doesn't need any sophisticated recipe, but even so, don't just condemn it to sausage and mash, good though it is. I like to see the great British banger served up with pride. Try this for a change.

You will need a pack of six Burnham Bangers, a can of sweetcorn, a pack of frozen peas and some potatoes. Boil the potatoes and mash with butter and milk. Warm up an oval serving dish while you are cooking the peas and sweetcorn separately. Fry the sausages until they are browned all round. Spread the mashed potato in the dish and lay the sausages side by side on the potato along the length of the dish, leaving a space between them. In these spaces fill alternatively with peas and sweetcorn so that you end up with sausage, peas, sausage, corn, sausage, peas, and so on. Of course you can ring the changes, as there are endless combinations that you can make.

Burnham-on-Crouch is a lovely little place nestling alongside the River Crouch. It is famous for its grade II listed building, The Royal Corinthian Yacht Club. It is a centre for yachting and, if you are there in August, you would be surrounded by several thousands of yachting enthusiasts, for it would be Burnham Week.

Further along Southminster Road you will come to The Limes Farm Shop on your left. It looks a bit like an old shed with lots of plants in terracotta pots all around the front door, but don't let that put you off, because it is more than a plant nursery. There is ample parking space in front, so there is no excuse for not stopping to have a look. You will not be disappointed.

Inside you will find a treasure trove of fresh produce, all grown on site, or from nearby. A truly Essex farm shop. In season they sell squash, courgettes, leeks, all grown on site. Their potatoes are from a local farm, as are their free range eggs. Fresh fruit is available in season and what is left after the season, you can buy frozen.

Walk through the shop and you will enter a large greenhouse full of herbaceous, bedding and basket plants. So you can kill two birds with one stone, stock up your garden and your kitchen. Also, around Halloween time, this is the place to come for pumpkins to delight or frighten the kids. However, if you do decide to visit, don't go on Monday, they are closed. Well, the staff have to spend some time growing the stuff!

So you've given in and bought a pumpkin for the Halloween celebration. You have scraped it out so that you can carve the face but now what do you do with the flesh? Don't throw it away, here's what you can do.

Cut the flesh into small pieces and place in a saucepan. Cover it with chicken stock. You can cheat and use a stock cube, but if you have your own stock, so much the better. Add a little salt and freshly ground black pepper. Bring to the boil and simmer until the flesh is very soft. Cut up a pack of cream cheese into small bits and put it in the soup. Liquidise and taste for seasoning. Serve piping hot with French bread on a cold Halloween night while staring at the face you've carved. To make it even more spooky, throw in a teaspoon of chilli powder.

As you drive along Southminster Road look out for the sign to Mangapps Railway Museum. This has to be one of Essex's curiosities.

This museum is really a private collection of railway paraphernalia put together by a devotee of all things railway. It is run by the Jolly family and is in fact their train set. Whereas we little boys had our train sets laid out on our bedroom floors, or if we were lucky, on a table specially provided in the attic by dad,(or was it for dad?) Mr Jolly's train set is life size and is laid out in his garden. It has a ¾ mile standard gauge, passenger carrying line with restored stations and signal boxes removed from various sites throughout Anglia. Operating on the line are ten steam and diesel locomotives and over eighty carriages. If you are a railway enthusiast, either diesel or steam, then this is the place for you. Go on, relive your youth; I did and it brought back memories of riding the GWR steam train to school. Have fun.

Dig deeper into the heart of the Dengie peninsular, an ancient fertile land that has stood the blasts from the North Sea for thousands of years. Fields that have grown asparagus since Roman times. Asparagus was known even before that. In fact, asparagus is depicted on an Egyptian frieze dated 3000BC. The Romans ate vast quantities of it, fresh in the spring and dried to eat later in the year. As the Romans settled in the Dengie peninsular I feel quite sure they cultivated asparagus in the same fields around Southminster that S. Thorogood & Sons do today. At New Moor Farm on Tillingham Road there are ten acres of the most delicious asparagus. From late April until about the middle of June, you may buy this wonderful vegetable from the farm gate. However, there is no pick your own. The bulk of the crop is sold to hotels, restaurants, and pubs and can even be found at various farmers' markets.

Mr Thorogood, who welcomed me to his farm with a warming cup of coffee on a cold morning, told me that in the cutting season, asparagus is cut every day and at the peak of the season, twice a day using just seven or eight people, most of whom come over every year from Europe. He shared with me his favourite recipe for cooking asparagus, which was simply to coat it in butter, wrap individual portions in foil and bake it in the oven for a few minutes. Put the foil parcels on a plate, open up the top, season to taste and enjoy.

What I like to do is steam it then shave some parmesan cheese on top. An alternative way is to sauté it quickly in butter with shavings of root ginger.

There are three types of asparagus, white, green and wild. The latter I once found in the hills around Valencia in Spain. It is a bit like bootlaces, long and thin with the tip being the ferrule on the end of the lace. It is an interesting plant that doesn't like to be picked or eaten. It grows under a very prickly bush and you must have a hooked stick to pull the plant aside to get at the asparagus. Apparently this is to stop the local sheep eating it.

On the B1021 just through Tillingham village, you will see a sign indicating Sarah Green's Organics. Ignore it, for Sarah is no longer there. She told me that not enough people shopped there to make it viable. I wasn't really surprised, as she was only open on Wednesdays. Keep on the road and turn in to Mark Road then follow the sign to Hall Farm.

Sarah is the third generation to run Hall Farm, where she grows all her own produce. To buy from her you must place a weekly order for a vegetable box which comes in five sizes from extra small to extra large. All the vegetables are seasonal and you get what you get. It may include, broccoli, cabbage, carrots, cauli, kale, leeks, onions and potatoes. I could go on, for it varies from season to season, but you name it, Sarah grows it. You can place an order in person, by phone 01621 778844 or e-mail at sarahgreen@farming.co.uk and she will deliver to you, provided you live within her local area. Don't expect to be able to pick up a one-off box on spec, you can't. If you do want to, you should go to Burnham-on-Crouch farmers' market on the third Sunday of the month or, if you live in London, Stoke Newington farmers' market. Other than that, make your way to Lathcoats in Galleywood, they stock Sarah's vegetables.

This thirty acre farm is truly organic, no chemicals are used whatsoever. Sarah relies on the ladybirds to deal with unwanted pests, such as aphids. As such it is a wonderful, natural habitat for wildlife. Groups of schoolchildren are welcome to visit the farm where they can learn how their food is grown and watch the kestrels at work.

Sarah told me that one of her winter favourites is her Crisp Winter Coleslaw. She has kindly allowed me to pass it on to you. This is how to make it. Finely slice a red cabbage and put in a mixing bowl, grate raw celeriac, carrot and finely chopped onion. Mix all the vegetables together and add a squeeze of lemon juice. Add black pepper, mayonnaise and mix well. But please use good mayonnaise, homemade or a luxury kind. Do not use salad cream. For such perfect, fresh vegetables, it deserves the best.

The B1021 snakes its way across what must be the remotest part of Essex, the Dengie Peninsular, which thrusts itself out into the North Sea, squashed between the Rivers Blackwater and Crouch. The road ends at the power station at Bradwell Waterside but don't go that far. When you get to the village of Bradwell on Sea, turn right on to a road that will take you to St Peter's Chapel. The road was built by the Romans to take their legionaries out to a fort, where the chapel now stands. It soon peters out and becomes a muddy track, which will lead you to St Peters-on-the-Wall. I left my car and walked the last few hundred yards, across marshy land, with the wind gusting straight off the North Sea, freezing my ears. Seagulls seemed to be motionless, just hanging on the wind, their screeching giving me an eerie warning of approaching the edge of the world. Up ahead was the tiny chapel, silhouetted against a grey sky.

The chapel is all that is left of a much larger church, built by St Cedd, a holy monk who came from Lindisfarne in AD 654 to bring Christianity to the Essex heathen. When the Romans were called back to Rome, their fort stood empty but not for long because the local tribes tore it apart and used the stone to build better houses for themselves. All that was left was the wall that once surrounded it. It was here that St Cedd built his church, using the stones from the wall, so hence it has become known as St Peters on the Wall. As you approach, although it is small, and only a fraction of the original, it is still very impressive being exactly as it was built over 1300 years ago and is well worth a visit.

Inside I was immediately impressed by the tranquillity of the place. I got a feeling of holiness, which was almost tangible, knowing that I was standing in England's oldest, still functioning church. It was almost devoid of furniture, which made its stark, stone walls bear witness to its antiquity. On a table by the door were spread little booklets and pamphlets detailing the chapel's history and the frequency of services held there. They were marked with their prices and there was an honesty box alongside. In such a place, who would dare to steal even a little booklet?

While you are on the Dengie peninsular, take the road from Bradwell to Steeple and look out for Gate Farm on the road. This is where Mrs Partridge will sell you some wonderful beef or lamb. For the last five years now, the Partridge family have been producing their meat, and selling retail from the farm gate. It is very much a family business, typical of Essex, where the husband is the farmer, father the butcher and Mrs Partridge herself, the management. They have a flock of about 500 sheep and a herd of 150 cows. I wonder why they couldn't have a herd of sheep and a flock of cows? Anyway, they are slaughtered locally and butchered back on site.

They will sell you a whole or half a lamb for the freezer or they will freeze it for you. Or, you can buy just one joint. Any sort of beef joint, even mince, is available. Provided you appear at the farm on a Friday 10 – 3 or Saturday 10 – 2, no order is too small. You can order by phone, 01621 772958 or online at www.steeplegate.co.uk and collect from the gate or they will deliver if you live in the Dengie area. Alternatively you can find their lamb at Great Garnets, Dunmow or the farmers' market at Burnham-on-Crouch and for their beef at Hadleigh.

While I was there, I was introduced to Caroline Wheeler who produces honey from her bees, which live on the farm. It would make a lovely baste for the lamb.

While I was talking with Mrs Partridge, she told me that her favourite way to cook a shoulder of lamb was slow roasting which she kindly allowed me to pass on to you. This is what you do. Place the shoulder in a flameproof casserole and seal it in a little hot oil. Remove and fry a chopped onion in the fat, then place some sprigs of fresh thyme or rosemary on the onion and place the meat on top. Now you can add almost anything you want, garlic, a little red wine or some honey. Cover and roast at 160c for three hours. I think that with my fan assisted oven I'd do it at 140c and then test it and maybe add another half hour if necessary.

Before leaving the peninsular, take the B1018 from Southminster and turn right into the village of Mayland. Here you will find Little Ashtree Farm where there is the one woman business of McLarens. Sandra makes soups. Yes soups, five unusually interesting varieties. You can choose from Mexican Hot Pot, Italian White Bean, Minted Pea and Lemon Grass or Red Onion, Burgundy, Sage and Thyme. You can order by telephone – 01621 741328 – or in person at Little Ashtree Farm, Mayland, Chelmsford. The soups are freshly brewed to order and come to you in mail-order cartons through the post. That is, unless your postman has missed his breakfast before his early morning round and decides he needs something absolutely delicious to keep him going. In which case, all you will get is an empty soup carton. However, if you don't trust your postman, you will find the soups at many farmers' markets throughout the county or in London at Marylebone and Borough markets.

4

Take the A414 out of Chelmsford, turn on to the B1010 and carry on until you reach the junction with B1018. At the crossroads keep straight on into Blind Lane and follow this until you come to Vicarage Lane on your right. Turn right and look out for Springstep Dairy at Mundon Hall Farm.

Bob Kirk, the farmer, proudly showed me his herd of 300 to 400 goats. I had never seen so many goats in one place before. I was glad they were behind a wire fence, but I needn't have worried, Bob explained that goats are not aggressive. A ram can be but only in the proper season when he is busy, jealously guarding his wives. They were housed in a large barn and appeared very clean and certainly very happy. Unlike sheep, goats are intelligent and inquisitive. As soon as they saw me, they all came running over to say hello. They poked their heads through the wire for me to stroke them. I remarked how friendly they were but Bob told me they were just hoping I had something for them to eat. They would even eat my sleeves if I let them. Goats would eat all day if they could, that is why feeding has to be regulated.

Bob showed me around the dairy where he turns his goats' milk into cream, yoghurt, ice cream, soft and hard cheese. I watched as the milk was churned into yoghurt under the most strict hygienic conditions. He sells his whole, semi and skimmed milk at various farmers' markets throughout Essex, including Burnham, Rochford and Leigh-on-Sea, but he will sell from the farm gate provided you go on Fridays, Saturdays or Sundays from 09.00 to 17.00. Why not give it a go.

Yoghurt makes a wonderful alternative to mayonnaise. Just add a little lemon juice to plain yoghurt and beat well. Otherwise, you can make a dressing with it. Mix equal amounts of plain yoghurt and olive oil, say about a quarter cup of each, one tablespoon of lemon juice, one crushed garlic clove and half a teaspoon of salt. Mix well and there you have it. By the way, did you know that mayonnaise originated in Mahon, the capital of the island of Menorca? Now there's a piece of trivia for you.

After leaving Mundon Hall farm, retrace your steps to the crossroads with B1018, turn left until the road makes a sharp left-hand turn. Hales Farm is immediately on your right. Here Mr Ferguson raises turkeys for Christmas. He buys five week old chicks from Kellys (Essex's largest turkey farm), and rears them ready for Christmas. They are fed on Mr Ferguson's own special feed, which makes their flesh taste so much better. After slaughter, they are hung for a week to ten days and they are ready for ordering in October. They come in Super Mini, size 10-13 lb and Broad Best at up to 28lb. The Super Mini is the perfect size for my miniscule appetite, for in the past I have ended up with a turkey big enough to feed an army. You can order by phone on 01621 742104 but have to collect from the farm, as Mr Ferguson cannot deliver. Don't turn up on Christmas Eve and expect to find a turkey if you haven't ordered one, because there will be none left. Hales Farm turkeys are not available at any farmers' market, nor in any shop. They are all sold at the farm gate, mainly to previous customers. They do not advertise in any journal, all advertising is done by word of mouth, the best advertising there is really. They are that good I recommend that you get your order in early.

I'll tell you what I do when cooking a turkey that perhaps you might like to try. Mash a chicken stock cube into some olive oil, or you can use softened butter if you prefer. Now lift the skin away from the flesh, gently with your fingers and spread the mixture under the skin all over the breast. Now replace the skin and pin it down with a skewer. Moisten the skin with a little oil or butter and season to your choice. Wash two large oranges and cut them up into six slices and lay them in the bottom of a roasting tin. Place the turkey on top. Roast in the usual way. When done, remove the turkey and keep warm, pour off any excess fat in the tin, add a chicken stock cube, the juice and zest of a lemon and a glass of dry white wine. Add enough hot water to reach your desired quantity. Bring to the boil, scraping off any bits stuck to the bottom of the tin. You can thicken the gravy with flour if you wish, but I never do.

Drive north on the B1018 towards Maldon on Fambridge Road. On the left you will come to Ben Rigby Game. You must stop and have a look, if you like game. When I went, Ben himself greeted me warmly and showed me around his unassuming premises. Not only does he sell game, as his name implies, but he has a wide selection of fresh fish. I asked him about the fish connection and he told me that he owns the very last working trawler out of Tollesbury. This little port, he strongly recommended me to visit, which I did. He does not work the boat himself but leaves it to his son. I couldn't help commenting that I thought it a wise decision. I noticed that among his wide variety of fish, I saw he had cod. I thought cod was now an endangered species but Ben assured me that North Sea cod was making a great comeback and the future looked good, provided the fishermen didn't fish too much. He agreed with me that it was a sin to throw back into the sea all cod caught over the legal limit. He suggested that some scheme should be in place whereby all cod, over the limit, should be handed over to some relevant authority in the port without any payment. It could then be distributed to various charities for the homeless and to schools.

The game on display in his cabinets was mind boggling. It included pheasants, partridges, grouse, wild duck, pigeons, rabbits, hare and venison. I fancied a grouse, but being just one day before the glorious 12th, the start of the grouse shooting season, all his grouse were last year's. I settled on a pheasant which was absolutely wonderful.

Not many of us have eaten grouse, but they really are quite delicious. The way I like them is this. You need two, or a brace, of grouse. Their skin must be oiled and traditionally you should use beef dripping. You can now get this in some supermarkets, but if you can't, mash half an oxo cube in a little softened butter and use that. Grease the birds all over, place in a roasting tin and cover with foil. Roast at 350f, gas 4, fan assist, 160c for about an hour. Take the birds out of the oven and joint them. Lay them on a serving dish. Melt some butter in a small pan, add about a tablespoon of fat from the roasting tin and any herbs of your choice. I often use powdered mace. Pour over the joints, cover and let them get cold.

There are literally hundreds of ways to cook game. I remember when I first cooked a wild duck, I roasted it as I would a chicken. It was so tough that even my dog found it hard to chew! Since then I always prefer to casserole them.

There's not much flesh on a wild duck so, for a family you'll need at least two. I make up a stock by boiling the giblets – they usually come with the ducks – in about one and a half pints of water, together with a stick of celery, an onion, a couple of carrots and a bay leaf. Simmer for about half an hour. Meanwhile rub the ducks all over with salt and cover the breasts with streaky bacon rashers. Put them in a roasting tin, fling in some chopped celery and roast for about half an hour on 375f, gas 5 or fan assist 160c. Then remove all the meat from the ducks and put in a casserole along with the chopped celery. Don't throw the bones away, keep for a future stock. Melt a little butter in a pan, add some flour and some stock that you have prepared, mix well and cook for a few minutes, then mix it with the rest of the stock, pour into the roasting pan, add a glass of red wine and boil rapidly for a few minutes. Then pour it over the duck meat in the casserole, cover and cook in the oven for up to an hour, until the meat is really tender.

Of course if you don't get the giblets, use chicken stock cubes, but where it says use one cube, use two. In any case, if you buy your ducks from Ben Rigby, you certainly will get the giblets.

There are fifteen vineyards in Essex and one of the largest and oldest is New Hall Vineyards. It is situated in the village of Purleigh on the B1010, just a little south of Danbury. When I visited, I was met by the owner, Piers Greenwood, who showed enormous patience in showing me around. He gave me a detailed account of the vines and the winery. He is a dedicated professional and really knows his craft. Foreigners tell us that England is not good at producing good wine but I can confirm that Piers has proved them wrong. The Romans were great consumers of wine and when they arrived in Britain, the wine they brought with them soon ran out. Now you couldn't keep a Roman army happy without their wine and the time it took to travel from Rome to England was far too long for them to wait. There was no DHL in those days. So what did they do? Planted some vines and produced their own wine, right here in Essex. In fact there are the remains of a Roman vineyard very close to New Hall.

As an experienced wine consumer, I can tell you that New Hall wines are excellent. Piers insisted I tried several and they were all, in their different ways, wonderful. He even insisted I accepted a couple of bottles to take away with me. Stephen Skelton says in his book, The Wines of Britain and Ireland, 'crops at New Hall must be amongst the best in the country'.

It is impossible for me to list here all the wines that New Hall produces, but amongst them are three excellent dry whites, three rosé wines and two wonderful medium/dry reds. They also produce a sparkling wine.

Every year in September, New Hall have a Wine Festival Arts and Crafts Open Day where you will find a craft fair, with demonstrations, an art show, wine tasting, and live music, including belly dancing. For the kids there is a story cave and a treasure hunt and even a bouncy castle. So while your kids are enjoying themselves, you can enjoy the wine, some seafood, tour the winery and find out how it's done. Having done that, if you fancy having a go yourself, you don't need to, for New Hall will lease you a row of vines for one year, so that you can become a proud vineyard owner of 80/90 established vines. These can produce between 220 to 320 bottles. They will even supply a personalised label. Now how good is that?

Now what do you do with a bottle of wine except drink it. Well here's an idea for you. Select a bottle of medium red wine, maybe Baccus. Ask for one that is young – the youngest you can get. Heat it very gently in a saucepan; do not let it boil. Add some gelatine leaves, or powder, and heat gently until the gelatine has completely dissolved. The label on the gelatine will give you the recommended quantities of liquid to gelatine. Pour into a basin and, when cold, put it in the fridge to set. To serve, turn it out of the basin, mash it up a bit with a fork and put spoonfuls of it on a plate with a good strong hard cheese and French bread.

After leaving New Hall, keep on the B1010 towards Chelmsford and look out for the signpost to the unusually named village, Cock Clarks. Here you will find a company, somewhat unusually situated deep in the leafy lanes of Essex, the Maldon Oyster & Seafood company. Based at Birchwood Farm, they are some six miles from the sea as the crow flies, but it might as well be a million miles, as the oyster swims. They raise their oysters, both native and rock, from the Goldhanger Creek, Heybridge. They bring them in to their premises at the farm where they are put through a thorough cleaning process lasting four and a half hours to remove any impurities. They are then supplied, alive of course, to many of this country's best restaurants and retailers.

This cleaning process is carried out in a barn-like structure and during my visit the two young men running the outfit were very welcoming but were concerned for my safety, urging me to take care as the floor was wet and very slippery. Indeed the whole building seemed to have a fair share of the North Sea in it. I discovered something about oysters: native oysters as well as mussels are only available when there is an 'R' in the month, whereas rock oyster are available all the year round. The Maldon Oyster & Seafood Company get through something like 20,000 oysters a week, but unfortunately you cannot buy them from the Birchwood Farm. You will have to seek them out from the top fishmongers throughout Essex but you won't have a problem.

There are many ways to eat oysters; probably the most popular way is raw with a squeeze of lemon juice. However served, they are quite delicious.

Stephen Pini, the Executive Chef of the Fishmongers Company and author of Simply Fish has very kindly allowed me to pass on to you his recipe for Chilli Coated Oysters. Follow his step by step guide and you will enjoy oysters at their very best.

This is what you will need. Twenty-four oysters (do not open until all of the ingredients and preparation is complete). 300ml of milk. Sunflower oil for deep frying. Salt and freshly ground pepper. four limes cut into wedges and chopped chives to garnish prior to serving.

For the salt and chilli coating – you will need, 175g plain flour, one teaspoon white pepper, two tablespoons chilli powder, one teaspoon monosodium glutamate (optional), one teaspoon oriental five spice powder, one red fresh chilli, deseeded and finely chopped, two tablespoons finely chopped coriander, two tablespoons chopped chives and one tablespoon Maldon sea salt.

For the red onion salsa – you will need, four tomatoes, deseeded and roughly chopped, one red onion finely chopped, one red chilli finely chopped, one clove garlic finely chopped, one lime, three tablespoons coriander finely chopped, three tablespoons olive oil, two tablespoons sweet chilli sauce and two tablespoons tomato ketchup.

Now this is what you do – first start the chilli coating by placing all the ingredients into a food blender, except for the salt flakes and blend into a homogenous mix, then remove and add salt flakes.

Now start on the onion salsa. Mix together all ingredients in a bowl, cover with cling film and place in fridge. (Adjust the seasoning when ready to serve).

Now open the oysters, remove the meat and place on a tray. Retain any liquid from the oysters and add it to the onion salsa mix.

Clean the empty oyster shells, dry and place on dishes ready to serve.

Heat the oil to 180 degrees (or follow the manufacturer's instructions for your deep fryer).

Place the milk in a small bowl and dip in the oyster, one by one then dredge them in the chilli coating.

Place the coated oyster on parchment paper. If you require a thicker coating, repeat the operation.

Once the oil has reached the required temperature, carefully lower in the oysters and cook for one to three minutes depending on their size. The oysters are cooked when they float and have turned golden brown and crispy.

Remove with a slotted spoon and drain on kitchen paper. It is best to cook the oysters in small batches and keep warm in a low temperature oven.

Place the oysters back in the half shells and put a small dish of salsa onto the serving plate. Garnish with a small wedge of lime, a little spoon of salsa on each oyster and chopped chives, before serving.

If you carry on the B1010 you will reach the A414, turn right and head for Woodham Mortimer. Dazilake Ltd is a small bakery situated on the main road just outside the village. The

A414 is a road that seems to go on forever and just when I had thought I had missed the bakery and was about to turn back, I found it. It was within a very small industrial complex. A sign at the entrance listed all the companies in the complex but the print was so small, it was impossible to read from a moving car. I parked and searched for Dazilake Ltd. I found a small roundel sign on one door which read 'Dazilake, cakes and comfort'. Anyway, you have no need to go to all this trouble because they do not sell retail from the bakery door.

I knocked and Susan Court, the owner, opened and invited me in. Susan is a very attractive young lady, originally from Kent but relocated here about seven years ago. She produces a lovely selection of cakes including brownies, shortbread, flapjacks, loaf cakes, lemon cakes and some biscuits. However, one of her specialities is a biscuit flavoured with lavender. It sounds very interesting and I am told tastes superb, consequently it has become very popular. Unfortunately, there are no lavender fields in Essex; perhaps some enterprising person should plant one, so giving Norfolk a run for its money. Anyway, the biscuit is made in Essex.

Dazilake's customer base is most impressive. For example, The House of Commons, Eurostar and Harrods to name but a few. For Harrods the products are with Harrods own label, an example of which I saw in the office. So next time you are whizzing under the channel to Paris, have a cup of tea and a Dazilake biscuit with it. However, if you do not intend to train it to Paris but you would still like to sample their cakes and comfort, you can buy them from many local farm shops, bakers, Meadowcroft, Wicks Manor and Lathcoats.

Susan told me that one of the most popular is chocolate brownie and I suspected that it was her favourite too. She has just started on a new innovation, which she is calling Childrens' Taster using oats and cranberries as well as other ingredients. I can't wait to see it on the market. Dazilake is an important company supplying some top people, without being at all grand. My visit was most enjoyable as was my sample of their loaf cake.

Loaf cake is very nice on its own, but it can be turned into a dessert. This is what you can do. Make a meringue by beating egg whites and sugar. Pipe individual pieces on to a non-stick baking tray, making them as flat as possible, like square biscuits. Put in a low oven and cook in the usual way. Meanwhile slice a loaf cake quite thinly. Beat some double cream until quite stiff and spread it on one side of two pieces of meringue. Then put a slice of the cake between the two biscuits.

Another idea is to slice a loaf cake, not quite so thin this time. Spread your favourite jam between two slices, making a sandwich. Pour custard or cream over it.

Make for Danbury and here you will find one of this country's leading turkey breeders. Kelly Turkeys on Bicknacre Road, Danbury has been rearing and supplying turkeys since 1972 when Derek and Molly Kelly opened up shop. Springate Farm came as a bit of a surprise to me, as I was expecting the traditional Essex farm, deep in the country near the village of Danbury. The buildings are modern, sparklingly clean and sit around a spacious car park. A sign directed me to 'Reception'. There I was greeted by Philip Regan, Sales & Marketing Manager. I explained my mission and he couldn't have been more helpful, giving me the company's history and the complete procedure from egg to table. Philip was obviously very proud of the company and, as I was to find out, rightly so. He handed me a couple of DVDs called 'Bred to be Wild'. One is a BBC documentary on turkeys, featuring several farms including Kellys. The other stars Philip Kelly, the son of the founders, showing how to cook and carve a turkey.

The list of the company's achievements, called 'Milestones in the Pursuit of Excellence' is long and impressive and includes a picture of Derek Kelly being awarded the MBE by the Queen in 1998. The company is very definitely geared up to do a lot of business in a modern way. It exudes an air of confidence and excellence that automatically shows you that you are in the presence of quality. Their promotional pack, which I was given not only included the DVDs but had leaflets on the Kelly Bronze Beef, the Kelly Bronze Chicken as was the 'Bred to be Wild' Kelly Bronze Turkey. It also had a guide to cuts of beef and how to cook it perfectly. All was presented in a card folder, so I came away with all the reading matter I needed, indeed everything except the turkey.

Some time ago the company celebrated its 25th anniversary and they are obviously very proud of it. I would describe the company as a leader in the game, having been described by the Daily Mail food tasting panel as 'the Rolls Royce of Turkeys.' Their range goes from hatch to despatch; the only thing they won't sell you is the egg. They are available from high class butchers throughout the country, from farmers' markets and many farm shops particularly in Essex. They even sell retail at the farm gate. You can order by phone on 01245 223581, in person at Bicknacre Road, or now online at www.kellysturkeys.com and they will deliver to your home or you can collect to save the delivery charge.

One thing that did surprise me during my visit to the site, I did not see a single turkey. They run wild in a nearby wood, so are completely free range. I would have thought that this might give a problem collecting the eggs, but I was assured that these clever birds know where their nesting boxes are and always use them. "Excuse me a minute, but I must just go and lay an egg!"

I have a little random information for you; it takes six to seven months for a bird to reach five kilos. At any one time, they have 30,000 breeding birds each laying four to five eggs each week. They are quickly placed on trays in an enormous incubator. They take twenty-eight days to hatch and 52% are female and 48% male. Over the Christmas period they sell 44,000 birds and your order must be in by the latest 18th or19th

December. They are not exactly cheap, but then neither is a Rolls Royce!

The company very kindly allowed me to reproduce the late Molly Kelly's way to cook the perfect Kelly Bronze Turkey. It is –

Remove the bird from the fridge and wash. Leave it to stand at room temperature for two hours before cooking. Place the turkey, breast down, in the roasting tin. Season the back of the bird with salt and pepper. Most of the fat deposits are on the back of the bird and they will percolate through the breast that will then cook in its own juices. Place a large peeled onion in the cavity for extra flavour. We do not recommend stuffing the bird, but to cook it separately. We do not recommend using tin foil, as you get a steamed skin not a crispy one. Preheat the oven to 180c (gas 4) before putting the turkey in. If you have a fan assisted oven and cannot turn off the fan, reduce the temperature to 160c. Turn the turkey over thirty minutes before the end of cooking time. This is easily done by holding the end of the drumsticks with oven gloves but be careful of the hot fat. Season the breast of the bird with salt and pepper. Place back in the oven and after fifteen minutes, take the bird from the oven and check the temperature by inserting a meat thermometer into the thickest part of the breast, or put a skewer into the thigh and when the juices run clear, the bird is done. If the juices are still pink, place back in the oven and check every ten minutes. Allow to stand for thirty to sixty minutes before carving.

The recommended cooking times are, two hours for a four kg bird and add a quarter of an hour for each extra kilo. This is without tin foil and no stuffing.

Follow this and you will not go wrong.

Now that you have cooked and eaten your turkey, you will have plenty of meat left. There are many recipes for leftover turkey, apart from cold with pickles, and one of my favourites is: Cut the turkey meat into small chunks, grate some cheese of your choice and cook some green beans. Boil some new potatoes and slice thinly when done. (If you can't get new, use salad potatoes). Now place a layer of potatoes on the bottom of a casserole. On the potato, put a layer of turkey meat, then a layer of green beans and then a layer of grated cheese. Continue these layers to the top, ending with a layer of potato. Take a tin of condensed soup, thin it with a little milk and pour over the casserole. Now spread some grated cheese on top and place the casserole, uncovered in the oven and bake for about twenty minutes or until the cheese is thoroughly melted.

While you are in Danbury, try to find Danbury Palace, which is one of Essex's best kept secrets. It lies alongside Danbury Park. It's a gothic pile built in the 16th century by Sir Walter Mildmay, Chancellor to the Exchequer to Queen Elizabeth I, who named it Danbury Place. The Mildmay family lived there until 1750. Since then it has changed hands many times. In the 19th century it became the home of the Bishop of Rochester, who renamed it Danbury Palace, as befitted a bishop. Since that time it has had four owners, the last of which turned it into a maternity home during the Second World War. Today, I understand it has been converted into several private apartments. I like to think that with so many different owners during 500 years, there must be many a ghost walking its lofty rooms.

5

Driving along the Goldhanger Road, the B1026, Heybridge to Colchester, I spied a sign on the left side saying Chigboro Smoke House. I was intrigued because in all my researches I had not come across it, so I turned in to a narrow lane, not much more than a dirt track, and eventually arrived at a yard, enclosed on three sides by farm buildings, one of which was labelled 'shop'. All over Essex you will find these, not very glamorous buildings but don't ignore them because you never know what you will find inside them. Inside this one, I found a most wonderful display of smoked foods; fish, flesh and fowl. There were duck breasts, cheese, trout, salmon, bacon; I could go on. Martin Balcomb is very much a one man band and is very enthusiastic in what he does. He showed me his two smoke holes, one for dry smoking and the other for hot smoking. The wood and sawdust he uses is all Essex oak. When I arrived, he had just lit the dry smoke hole and the smell was enticing.

All his products for smoking are sourced locally in Essex wherever possible. As well as his smoked products, Martin also sells homemade marinades of various kinds and flavoured olive oils. He sells retail from his shop and is open Tuesdays to Saturdays, 09.00 to 17.00. He also shows at the market in Loughton High Street on the first Sunday in the month and at Barleylands, Billericay, 2nd and last Saturdays in the month.

Martin's smoke house was so genuine, he is so devoted to producing good, honest smoked food that I could hardly stop myself from buying. I bought some smoked trout, smoked salmon and some marinated hot smoked salmon. The marinade was a combination of olive oil, thyme, muscovado sugar and citrus. It was absolutely delicious as were all the other items that I sampled. His small enterprise is a perfect example of what is the best of Essex and one of which the county should be proud. I can't wait to pay another visit and buy. I sincerely recommend you to go there.

There are very many things that you can do with smoked fish, eaten raw or cooked. One of the things I like is to make is a smoked salmon spread; pate is too posh a word for it. All you do is put some smoked salmon into a food processor and while running it, add pieces of butter until it resembles a smooth paste of the consistency you like. Then grind some black pepper into the mixture and add some lemon juice. Taste it from time to time until it is to your taste. Turn out into a bowl and add a few pieces of chopped up smoked salmon and mix well. Put the mixture into a pate dish and decorate with a slice of lemon. Put it in the fridge to set.

This is delicious on toast or spread over chicory leaves or on sticks of celery. To ring the changes, reduce the quantity of butter and replace it with cream cheese. In this case you must make sure that it is thoroughly chilled before serving.

After leaving Chigboro Smoke House carry on into Maldon. I suppose the fame of Maldon rests upon its salt. However, there is a lot more to this hilltop town than that. From the town centre you are not immediately aware of the town's connection with the sea. The busy High Street is like many others in market towns all over the country, but here the gentle downward slope will bring you eventually to Hythe Quay where the River Blackwater meets the North Sea. Tied up here are the old Thames Barges. They are all kept in excellent condition, reminding us of days long gone. They are no longer in use for carrying goods to London, they are now employed for educational purposes and leisure. They are very rarely seen on the Thames today but I remember there used to be one moored by Wandsworth Bridge in London but I think that has now gone.

Maldon is one of the oldest towns in Essex. In fact in Saxon times there were only two towns in the county, Maldon and Colchester. The Romans were here in the year 45AD and it is known they started producing salt from the sea and raised oysters in the area. Little is known before that but it is believed that it was an important settlement but lost its importance when the Romans made Colchester their capital. After the Romans left, the Saxons settled in the area. They remained, presumably undisturbed until AD 991 when the Vikings invaded and a great battle took place in Maldon. The Saxons lost and the site is now an international historical site marked by a plaque. If you want to find out more about the town, there is a wonderful collection of its archives in the Maldon Museum housed in the former market hall in the High Street. Another interesting place to visit is The Museum in the Park in Mill Road, which has a collection of old Maldon shop fronts, a fire engine and a 1940s living room as well as a Victorian parlour.

But perhaps Maldon's greatest claim to fame is its sea salt. Housed in modern offices is the headquarters of one of Essex's most famous companies, The Maldon Crystal Salt Company. Famous all over the world as the producers of Essex sea salt. As well as the regular sea salt flakes, the company now produces natural rock salt and a very new product, smoked sea salt. Oh, and what goes together with salt? Well pepper of course. They now import peppercorns from India and sell them to us. All The Maldon Crystal Salt Co's products are found in most supermarkets and good grocers everywhere.

Sea salt has been produced here certainly since Saxon times, but it is believed that the Romans actually evaporated the sea to produce sea salt in their time and the Domesday Book lists forty-five salt pans in the Maldon area. Salt is still produced in the old way in the Blackwater Estuary. Salt crystals form on seawater as it evaporates and although the method remains the same, the tools of the trade have changed.

Many chefs and cookery writers claim that sea salt is the best to use and Maldon sea salt the best of the lot. Unfortunately you cannot visit the salt pans, but if you want to know more, log on to www.maldonsalt.co.uk and you will find out all you want to know.

Some ideas of what to do with salt.

Joint a chicken and lay the pieces on a bed of sea salt then cover them completely with more salt. Bake for about an hour and ten minutes. Break open the salt casing, brush off the joints, serve hot or cold. You can leave the chicken whole but this needs a lot more salt, or you can do a whole fish this way.

Sea salt makes a good brine – take four cups of dark beer – Guinness or real ale, half a cup sea salt, half a cup brown sugar, a quarter cup of pickling spice, a quarter teaspoon of cayenne pepper. Bring all the ingredients to the boil until the sugar and salt have melted. Allow to cool. Lay a trout in this brine for about two hours before grilling.

Maldon has a dish specifically named after it. It is called Maldon Boiled Beef, which is the copyright of J.Salmon Ltd. of Severnoaks, Kent, who have very kindly allowed me to reproduce it here for you. You will need a piece of topside or silverside, one carrot, scrubbed, one onion, peeled, two cloves of garlic and a bunch of fresh herbs of your choice. This is what you do: Place the meat in a saucepan with the vegetables and herbs, cover with water. Bring to the boil then simmer till meat is tender. To serve, slice the meat and sprinkle it with sea salt.

When you leave Maldon, take a trip up the B1019 Hatfield Road and stop off at the Museum of Power. Now I realise that this doesn't sound the most exciting place in the world but, wait a minute, it's well worth giving it a try.

It is housed in the Essex/Suffolk water authorities' old steam pumping station, which was built in the 1920s to supply water to Southend. It's strange isn't it that Southend is on sea and they have plenty of seawater. In Malden, they are busily extracting salt from the sea and you would think that if they took enough salt out, the water would be left drinkable. So why didn't Southend do that? Anyway, something must have happened because the pumping station was shut down in 1963. So where does Southend get its water from now? The pumping station became a scheduled ancient monument and turned into the museum. A monument built in the 20s and pronounced ancient? In that case in another ten years, I'll be an ancient monument.

The museum has a wonderful collection of old machinery, equipment and bygones of an earlier age. It includes a miniature railway offering rides, a model village and railway, a riverside nature trail, a tea room and shop. They tell me that in the grounds you will be able to catch sight of kingfishers, woodpeckers, egrets and even otters; that is if the steam train doesn't frighten them all away. Why not give it a go for there are plenty of things to interest your children and, I suspect, Dads will be intrigued as well.

Now if it is a nice sunny day, a good place to go is nearby Heybridge Basin. It is one end of the Chelmer & Blackwater Navigation Canal and was dug out in 1793. It runs for thirteen miles to Chelmsford. It allowed lighters, carrying cargo off the ocean-going clippers to carry their goods up to town, via a sea lock, which is still there. It's a good place to visit to have a rest after a busy sightseeing tour. You can enjoy a bite to eat and a drink sitting on the terrace by the lock outside the pub, The Old Ship. If you enjoy real ale, this is the place to go.

Just beyond Maldon I drove along the B1026 in the direction of Tolleshunt D'Arcy looking for Wharf Road. By the time I reached the Domesday Book village, I realised I had somehow missed it. Driving back slowly, skirting the Blackwater estuary, I knew why I hadn't found it, because it wasn't there. I pulled in to a caravan site, opposite the tiny Osea Island and enquired. They directed me to the so-called Wharf Road which was a couple of yards further on. It kept its identity secret, wore no sign. It wasn't so much a road, more of a track. I found myself in a little enclave of what looked to me to be a group of tarted up huts. The numbering of the houses was almost non-existent and it proved impossible to find No.21, the address I was looking for. Eventually I came across a lady who was mowing, what appeared to be the entire village green – that's flattering it - and she pointed out the house of Miss Stoneham's Preserves, No. 21.

The area in front of the house looked a mess. I was told that the Gas Board were digging a gas main at the time, so I forgave the untidiness. There were steps up to the front door, for the house was built on a hillside overlooking the water. There were stilts propping up the house, stopping it from falling into the estuary. It looked precarious to me. Miss Stoneham appeared to be very pleased to see me, invited me into her kitchen and insisted on making coffee. She is typical of what is called a Cottage Industry, all her products homemade by herself in that very kitchen. Her range of products is large and how she could produce them all in such a small space, I could not understand. But she does, without help and I was very impressed.

Miss Stoneham's main products are chutneys, pickles, jellies, jams and marmalades and, from what I was told by the local people, were absolutely delicious. The range is too big to list here, but just a few are Lime Pickle, Pear Pickle, Pumpkin Chutney, Beetroot Chutney, Quince Jelly, Tarragon Jelly, Raspberry Jam and Ginger Curd. You should go to her website at www.miss-stonehams-preserves.co.uk for the complete list.

She sells mostly wholesale and her products look very countrified, with pretty coloured cotton tops to the jars, with simple black and white labels. She has been in business since 1990 and is obviously doing very well. She is again a good example of what I found all over Essex, creative people doing excellent business. She does sell at some farmers' markets but unfortunately, none in Essex. On the fourth Saturday each month, she sells at South Kensington market and at Blackheath which, she says, is much more successful. However, she will sell retail through the post but it is better to order more than one jar, postage is quite expensive. The more you buy, the cheaper the delivery. Contact her at Miss Stonehams Preserves, 21 Wharf Road, Mill Beach, Maldon, CM9 4QY. She really deserves your support.

Before leaving the area, I had another word with the lawn-mowing lady. She told me that all the houses in Wharf Road were placed here by her grandfather who transported them, bit by bit from the nearby Osea Island. They had been billets for the military on the island during World War Two. So, my description of tarted up huts wasn't far from the mark, but very attractive they are and what a position!

I was trying to think of interesting things to do with Miss Stoneham's Preserves but they are obviously so good, they don't need much. One of her products did give me an idea. She has a garlic and chilli Jelly. Go out and buy some Mexican tortillas, the soft kind; you can get flour or corn ones, doesn't matter. Chop up a tomato into large pieces, lay some in the middle of a tortilla, add some of Miss Stoneham's garlic and chilli jelly and wrap the tortilla around it. There you have a Fajita. You can do this with many of her products. Why not try her North Indian Lime Pickle in a tortilla on its own?

Just outside Tolleshunt Major, on Witham Road, you will find perhaps one of the very best farm shops in Essex. Wicks Manor Farm for me was a wonderful find. I was greeted warmly by Mary Howie, shown around her excellent shop and invited in to the house for a chat. Wicks Manor is run by Mr and Mrs Howie and their two sons. The farm has about 250 acres that support around 2000 pigs that live in what in the pig world could only be described as five star accommodation. From what I observed, each pig, whilst not exactly a pet, is very much loved by the family. They produce what I think must be the very best pork products in the county. They sell pork, bacon, gammon, ham and sausages, all produced on the farm. Apart from their own products, the shop stocks local Essex produce like Marriages flour, Tiptree jams, Dazilake cakes and Maldon sea salt. Everything was so well displayed, I was tempted to buy the lot.

Wicks Manor has another surprise up its sleeve in the shape of the quaintly named Shaken Udder Company. This is an outfit run by other members of the Howie family, Andrew and Jodie. They make milkshakes – hence Shaken Udder. When I was there they were producing only four flavours, strawberry, banana, chocolate and strawberry cheesecake. By now they may well have added other flavours to the range. You'll find them all in the shop but if you ever find yourself in Waitrose in Colchester, they stock them.

OK, so you've bought a gammon joint from Wicks Manor Farm, congratulations, you've got one of the best. You can either bake it or boil it. It can be either smoked or unsmoked; the former seems to have a stronger flavour. Some people recommend that you should soak the joint overnight in cold water, or bring it to the boil, throw away the water and start again. This is only necessary if you require a less salty taste. To boil a gammon allow twenty minutes for 500g plus twenty minutes. I always allow it to cool down in its water. To bake it, allow thirty minutes per 500g plus fifteen minutes. I mostly bake mine, sticking it with cloves and add a bay leaf. Wrap it loosely in foil, opening the foil for the last fifteen to twenty minutes. When boiling a gammon, fling in an onion and a couple of carrots, plus whole black peppercorns. You can serve it with parsley sauce. Now you can buy this in a packet, but be generous to your gammon, make your own. It's easy, just white sauce and chopped fresh parsley. This way you will enjoy the gammon at its very best.

Oh and by the way, Wicks Manor has another secret. The 17th century moated manor house offers bed and breakfast. After a long day touring the county, enjoying its food, why not stay there and enjoy the best English breakfast that there is.

Now you should make for Mersea Island. Take the B1025 and cross over to the island on the causeway known as The

Strood. Go as far as you can, through West Mersea town, turn right on to the sea front and continue until you can go no further. On your left you will find the Company Shed restaurant – sorry, eaterie. Looking unpretentious and shed-like, go in for the best, freshest fish and seafood you will ever have eaten. You can't book a table, so go early or queue up and wait. This world famous restaurant is owned by Richard Haward's wife and relies on what her husband pulls out from the sea. It is really a fishmongers with tables and, except for the seafood and the knives and forks, you will need to bring anything else you require with you.

Richard's family have been growing oysters on 15 acres of the West Mersea Creek since the 18th century. In fact oysters were discovered way back by the Romans and they have been grown there ever since. Essex is justly famous for its fish and seafood, having over 400 miles of coastline, the longest in England and the oysters and fish don't come any fresher than from Richard Haward and the Company Shed because they are only inches from the sea. Richard's oysters are sold mainly through wholesalers but you can buy them from the Company Shed or Borough Market in London or from Ken Green in Clacton.

When visiting West Mersea you must remember two things. One – the local oysters, called natives, are only available when there is an R in the month, presumably from September to April. Two – during high Spring tides, the causeway is flooded by the sea so you have to wait for low tide to get on or off the island.

There are many ways of eating oysters, apart from the obvious, raw straight out of their shells and here is what you can do.

The simplest is Angels on Horseback. Wrap each oyster with a piece of bacon, secure with a wooden toothpick and bake in the oven for ten to twelve minutes until the bacon is crispy. They are best eaten hot. Or, they can be roasted in their shells. Just plonk them in a baking pan and roast on high until the shells open. Open them up completely, be careful not to burn your fingers, and serve in their shells. You could sprinkle with salt and pepper or any spice you desire. Even a little grated parmesan cheese would be good.

One of my favourite ways to eat oysters is in a champagne sauce, which I had once in the Ritz. I don't know how they did them but what I do is this. Make your sauce by melting three tablespoons of butter in a saucepan and blend in three tablespoons of flour. Then add half a cup of chicken stock very gradually. When blended in add half a cup of double cream and half a cup of champagne. Stir and simmer moderately for about ten minutes. Place oysters in their open shells in a grill pan, coat liberally with the sauce and grill for about two minutes. This would do for about twenty-four oysters, so you should adjust your quantities to the number of bivalves you have. You don't have to use champagne, of course, you could use any dry sparkling wine, i.e. Cava.

Drive over to the other side of the island, East Mersea. On Rewsalls Lane you will find one of Essex's smallest vineyards, Mersea Island Vineyard & Brewery. The Barbers have been producing wine here for over twenty years. Father seems to run the winery and the son, the brewery. That seems to be about the correct delineation of responsibility. English wines are growing in acceptability and there is no reason why not. After all, the Romans decided that Essex soil could produce good vines and they certainly knew a good wine when they drank it. So not only did they introduce us to oysters, wine too it seems. Unfortunately when they left, they seem to have taken wine growing with them. Although there is some evidence of wine production in England after that, it wasn't until the 50s that wine became a commercial proposition and not until about ten years later that wine growing returned to Essex.

Mersea Island produces five wines, four white and one rose. Their sparkling you could perhaps use in your champagne sauce but to drink with your oysters, perhaps their

Mersea Native would be the one. Another of their dry white wines is called Mersea Mehalah. I was curious about the name. It is named after the heroine of a tragic love story written by a local vicar of the 19th century, the same man who wrote the hymn, 'Onward Christian Soldiers'. I did try their Island Rose wine, which would be great to drink on a warm, sunny day in the garden.

The brewery side of the business produces cask and bottle beers. Island Oyster at 5.1% ABV is the one they suggest you drink with oysters. However, it's quite strong and after several, I suggest you should book into one of their B & B rooms right there on site, so you won't have to drive.

While you are in East Mersea, at Pyefleet Quay on East Road you will find Colchester Oyster Fisheries Ltd. This company is probably one of the United Kingdom's biggest suppliers of oysters. Their oyster beds in the Pyefleet Channel date back to the 12th century but the company is relatively modern, only being here since 1964.

Graham, who met me at the door, took me upstairs to the boardroom from where, through large panoramic windows, I could see the complete expanse of the oyster beds. I looked out over the tranquil water where nothing seemed to be happening but, under the surface there lived an enormous colony, almost a city, of oyster activity. These beds produce, in season, something like 35,000 oysters per week!

Unfortunately, you can only buy from the company online at info@colchesteroysterfishery.com where you can order oysters, crab, lobster and scallops and they will deliver to you. Otherwise you will have to dine at some of this country's grandest restaurants to enjoy Colchester Fisheries' oysters.

Eat your oysters raw, or if you must, take them out of their shells, put a smidgen of their juice in a ramekin, put the oyster on top, a dash of crème fraiche mixed with your favourite cheese, grated and slip them under a hot grill for a few minutes. Delicious.

Now if you can't get off the island because of the high tide, spend your time at Cudmore Grove Country Park. It is in Bromans Lane, at the far end of the island at East Mersey. Go any further and you will fall into the sea. This is probably one of Essex's more spectacular parks, being situated where it is, looking out over the North Sea.

There is so much to see and do there. For instance, as this is in such a strategic position, it became a lookout for approaching enemies during world war two. The remains of England's defences can still be seen. Essex County Council purchased the site in 1979 to preserve a piece of Essex for the people to enjoy. I have to tell you that they succeeded. You can spend hours bird watching, both of the land and sea varieties. The wildlife there includes small mammals, lizards, insects and fifteen types of butterfly. Walk along the coastal cliffs for an invigorating breath of North Sea air and if that has given you an appetite, the café will supply a whole range of light refreshments. Cudmore Grove is guaranteed to blow your cobwebs away.

6

On the Mersea Road, just south of Abberton you will come to the Butterfly Lodge Dairy, run by Warren and Ellie Goff. Their interest is mainly in goat. They sell the meat and from the goats' milk they make cheese and ice cream. Known under its brand name 'Caprilatte' the ice cream comes in forty flavours and is quite delicious, I can tell you. As well as goat, the farm produces some beef, lamb and pork. As far as I could tell, their pork is unique in that it comes from a special little pig called a Kune Kune. This is a Maori word meaning fat or plump. Obviously this pig originated in New Zealand, but there are several breeders now in this country. There is even a Kune Kune Pig Society. It is a much smaller pig, being only about twenty-four inches high. The meat, I am told, is very succulent, although I have never eaten it. The pigs are in great demand as pets, as they are small, friendly and seem to like us humans. In which case, I don't know if I would want to eat one.

The Butterfly Lodge also has an education centre which Ellie controls. This is a school that runs courses in animal welfare and general farming, mainly for school children, including some with learning difficulties. The courses last from a few weeks up to a year and I believe are well attended.

In all, a very enterprising outfit right in the heart of Essex.

My favourite restaurant in Mexico City is 'La Ribera' where they specialise in goat. It comes cooked in many different ways, but my favourite is 'Cabrito'. This is a whole kid goat, roasted and then chopped up into pieces and piled on a platter for you to serve yourself with your fingers. If you fancy it, this is what you do. Buy a small kid from Butterfly Lodge, if they will sell you one, and have them prepare it for the oven. When you get home, wash it well and dry it thoroughly. Melt some butter in a pan and combine it with a good quality olive oil. Crush up as many garlic cloves as you like and mix into the butter/oil. Warm it gently, do not allow it to boil, but just enough to extract the maximum flavour from the garlic. Then smear this all over the kid and place in a slow oven at say, 250f; 130c; gas half or 120c fan assisted oven for up to 4 hours. Place a heatproof dish of water in the bottom of the oven, which will keep the meat moist. During cooking, check from time to time and baste if necessary and top up the water. It is done when a skewer goes into the meat easily. Take it out of the oven and let it rest, during which time, make up the gravy using the bits in the roasting tin. Use a thickening agent if you want the gravy to be thick so that you can dip the pieces of meat into it rather than pour it. Chop it up into manageable lumps and enjoy. I recommend drinking a gutsy red wine with El Cabrito.

In Mexico they also eat it casseroled or Cazuela. Select a shoulder joint which you can either cook whole or cut up. I usually cut it up into casserole pieces. Sear the meat in hot fat on all sides and place in a casserole dish on a bed of carrots, or any root vegetable you prefer. Lay a bunch of fresh coriander on top. Chop up a good Spanish onion and place around the inside of the casserole. Chop up some garlic cloves – as many as you dare – very finely. Now select a chilli pepper. If you don't want it too hot, choose a Poblano or, a little hotter, a Jalapeno or very hot, a Habanero but do be careful. Chop up the pepper; you can either include the seeds or leave them out, in which case the heat will be reduced. Scatter the chopped pepper and garlic over the meat. Season with salt and pepper and cover with water. Bring to the boil and then simmer until the meat is very tender. Buen Provecho.

On Abberton Road, near the quaintly named village of Fingringhoe, keep your eyes peeled for a house called 'Clay Barn'. In it you will find a most charming couple, Charles and

Shirley Trollope. It is a lovely house, not a bit like a barn at all but is set in an orchard of some very interesting trees. Charles and Shirley have preserved something of old England: they grow quinces.

They welcomed me warmly into their house and insisted that I had a cup of tea while explaining what they do. Originally they grew apples but they found the market so competitive, they chopped down their trees and planted fruit trees of a lesser competitive variety, quince. Like me, I suppose you have no idea what a quince is, nor what it is used for but Shirley soon explained. The quince is basically a Mediterranean fruit and is very ancient. Known to the Romans but unknown in England until the time of Elizabeth I. We are told that it was the favourite fruit of Charles II and also, that William of Orange sent a quince to London as the signal that he had landed.

The quince is harvested from the end of September to the end of October. Most of their produce is sold to Wilkins, Essex famous jam maker, however you can buy from Clay Barn provided you place your order before the end of October. Once you have your quinces, what to do with them? Shirley gave me several recipes which she very kindly allowed me to share with you. They can be made into jelly, marmalade, jam and chutney and even into wine or liqueur. One that interested me is Quince Tarte Tatin. This is what you do.

Brush the inside of a 7-8 inch sponge tin with melted butter. Line the base with greaseproof paper and brush with more melted butter and sprinkle brown sugar over the paper and press down. Make pastry in your usual way, or buy it readymade, roll out and cut to the size of your sponge tin. Peel, core and slice one large or two medium quinces. Gently poach in a mixture of honey and water until partly cooked. Arrange in circles over the sugar and put the pastry circle on top and press down. Bake in the centre of the oven at 180c or 350f degrees for about 30 minutes. Cool, turn out upside down and eat while still warm.

Another recipe that caught my eye was called Membrillo. To make it you roughly chop about 4 lbs quinces and stew with ½ pint water until soft. Sieve and weigh the pulp. Boil with an equal quantity of sugar until the paste leaves the sides of the pan. Stir continually to prevent burning – also wrap your hand in a cloth because it bubbles and spits. Pour into flat trays lined with greaseproof paper and leave in an airing cupboard, or the bottom of an Aga, for three or four days. When completely firm like Turkish Delight, cut into small pieces, roll in caster or icing sugar. Store between greaseproof paper in airtight tins.

Clacton-on-Sea is probably the most popular seaside resort on the east coast. Until the onset of cheap air travel and package tours to overseas destinations, Clacton was a very popular holiday resort with the English. However, in recent years, tourist numbers have declined but now, Clacton seems to be making a comeback. It seemed to me that the town has had a complete spring clean and the seafront and pier are very pleasant.

Just outside the town, on Stephenson Road, is a family business that might be said to be in a bit of a pickle. Vineyard Fine Foods, who also own Bromley's Pickle Company, produce a large range of chutneys, pickles and relishes under the Vineyard label and, under the Bromleys label, jams, marmalades and some exotics like sticky onion chutney or tomato and chilli jam. All their recipes are their own and are gluten and dairy free and suitable for vegetarians.

Pender Richardson, the owner, told me that they started out in 1999 in a small delicatessen in Colchester. They moved into their present, modern premises in 2004 and since then the business has expanded rapidly. Everything is hand made using, where possible, Essex grown vegetables but things like mango have to be imported. They can turn out 1200 jars a day and supply to the likes of Tesco and the Co-op as well as some well known names in the hamper market. Look out for their simple, eye catching labels in Asda in Colchester and Chelmsford and many other local stores. You won't be disappointed.

The area around Clacton used to be made up of four villages. Clacton-on-Sea, Great Clacton, Little Clacton and Great Holland. This has now amalgamated into one urban area. It is difficult to see where one ends and another begins. It was Great Holland that I was after, where the Park Fruit Farm is located. It is a maze of tidy streets and houses, a sign of the prosperity of the area. Park Fruit Farm is on Pork Lane off the B1033 which, according to the local map, runs between Frinton and Weeley but takes so many twists and corners, without directions, it is very easy to get lost, as I did. However, I found it in the end and you should too.

Park Fruit Farm grows thirty-eight varieties of apples and the great thing is that they are all English. I get tired of seeing so many foreign imported apples in the supermarkets these days, when England used to produce so many superior varieties. So, if you like a good English apple, Park Fruit Farm is for you. They also grow four varieties of pears and nine of plums and, in the summer/autumn season, raspberries and blackberries.

As my visit was unannounced, I was unable to meet the owner, Stephen Elsworth but I did manage to have a chat with him on the telephone. He told me that his orchards were originally planted in 1935 and now cover over thirty acres. It is a family run concern, now into its third generation. Most of the fruit grown is sold in the farm shop, which also stocks locally grown vegetables and other local products such as Wilkins jams, Marriage flour and yes, even Williamsons frozen fruit. One of the products of which they are proud, is their apple juice. This is pure apple with absolutely nothing added. It will freeze, otherwise keep it in the fridge for up to five days only, after that it will start to ferment. At the back of the shop there is a little tea room-come-restaurant, but if you do decide to eat there, don't be in a hurry.

Stewed apple is the first thing that springs to mind when thinking about apples or perhaps apple sauce for pork roast. You can tart these up a bit by throwing in your favourite spice when stewing apples such as cinnamon, star anise or mixed spice. On the other hand you can shave off some pieces of root ginger and add to the apples. Instead of apple sauce, try Apple rings. What I do is cut a cooking apple into slices, leaving the peel on, then take out the core. Place them in a bowl, cover them with brandy and sprinkle liberally with sugar. Keep in the fridge overnight. Next day, make up a simple batter using beer, dip the slices into it and dust them both sides with a mixture of caster sugar and cinnamon powder. Fry until golden and serve surrounding your roast pork.

One of the very best fruit combinations I know is blackberry and apple. I have often wondered why they go together so well, they seem to be made for each other. The answer is simple, they ripen at the same time of the year. Before the days of deep freeze, people could only use what was in season. There is nothing nicer than a blackberry and apple pie or crumble. A marriage made in heaven.

Now if all this talk of recipes and food has made you want to do some cooking but you might like a little professional help, go to Coastal Foods, Ashlyns House, 83 Forth Avenue, Frinton-on-Sea. Jo Beattie and her husband Brian run a cookery workshop where they offer three separate sessions that you can join. One is a demonstration where you can watch Brian do all the cooking; the second is Demo and Dine, where Brian cooks a three course meal and then you can eat it. The third session consists of a proper workshop where you do the cooking with the help of master chef, Brian Beattie.

This husband and wife team have been running the business for over three years since they closed their restaurant in Frinton. They do not advertise, their fame spreads by word of mouth. If you don't fancy doing the cooking but would just like to have an excuse to look around, you may buy a bottle of their award winning French Dressing, which they make using locally grown rapeseed oil and take the opportunity to have a nose around; they won't mind. You can contact them on 07971100704 or at coastalfoods@tiscali.co.uk

While you're in the area, have a drive along the coast to Walton-on-the-Naze. The Naze is one of our many interesting peninsulars of the North Sea coast, which is the site of a unique tower. Built in the 18th century, this 86ft structure was built as a navigational aid to shipping. It wasn't exactly a lighthouse, although it did once sport a beacon. However, it is widely believed to be the predecessor of the lighthouse and is the only one of its kind in the world.

Now privately owned, it is open to the public. It houses an art gallery showing paintings by local artists – all of which are for sale, a gift shop, a tearoom and a viewing platform. To get up to the platform you have to navigate a spiral staircase of 111 steps. But, they say, when up there the view is spectacular. In other words, it's worth the climb. You should hurry though because the cliff on which the tower stands is eroding fast. In fifty years it will have tumbled into the sea. So if you want to see it, be quick.

It may just be that you are on your way to Harwich, perhaps to catch a ferry to Holland. If so, stop off at Tendring where you will find Gleeds Emporium. An interesting little shop which is more than the village shop and post office, it is also a delicatessen and it specialises in gift hampers. Now, if you are planning to visit your auntie in Holland and want to take her a gift, you could do a lot worse than a gift hamper. If you telephone them in advance on 01255 830423 they will make one up for you consisting of typically English produce, perfectly suitable for the Dutch.

From Tendring take a small country road to the A133 and turn off to the village of Great Bentley. On St Mary's Road you will find another of Essex's interesting farm shops, Carpenters. The farm incorporates over 130 acres of arable land growing potatoes, asparagus, raspberries, strawberries and gooseberries. They have a large pick your own section, which over the years has grown from farm gate sales to a purpose built farm shop. They also have an impressive display of Essex produce, including meat and fish as well as a range of frozen produce out of season. Carpenters Farm Shop is a small, family run business, typical of Essex which is well worth a visit.

Buy some raspberries and strawberries and make what I call, Strasberry Pies. Although the real strasberry is not a hybrid between strawberry and raspberry, it is a variety of wild strawberry with a raspberry flavour. It was introduced into this country from Holland some time ago, but as far as I know, it is not grown in Essex. This is what you do. Boil together sugar and water, add a teaspoon of mixed spice powder. When syrupy, add your raspberries and strawberries. If the strawberries are large, cut them up so that your fruit is about the same size. Coat in the syrup very well. Leave to cool. Roll out puff pastry and cut into 6" squares. Put a little of the fruit in the centre of the squares and fold over, corner to corner making triangular pies. Don't forget to damp the edges to make them stick. Press tight. Brush them with milk or beaten egg and bake at 180c for 20 minutes until they are nice and brown.

On your way back to Colchester on the A133, you will pass the village of Frating. This is salad country. Here Anglia Salads Ltd have fields and fields of salads growing. They grow every type of lettuce, including the red sort but strangely enough, they don't grow Iceberg, which I would have thought was the most popular lettuce there is. You have no need to go there because they do not sell retail. They sell their entire crop to processors. You know when you walk into a supermarket to buy some salad, but can't be bothered to wash it and tear it into bits but buy it already washed and prepared in a little plastic bag, well the odds are, that it came from Anglia Salads. So next time you buy a bag, think Essex.

Here's something you can do. Buy a bag of salad and tip it into a salad bowl. Add some dried fruit, apricots, bananas, apples or a mixture. Make a dressing; my favourite is three spoons of extra virgin olive oil, one spoon of lemon juice. Spoon size depends on how much dressing you need. Add a pinch of salt, a pinch of sugar and a quarter teaspoon of mustard powder. Mix well, preferably by shaking it in a sealed jar and pour it over the salad when ready to serve.

Before arriving back in Colchester, you will pass the Beth Chatto gardens in Elmstead Market. If you are into visiting gardens, then Beth Chatto is one of the very best. Although it is a plant nursery as well as a garden, you will have to pay to get in. But if you can persuade them that all your children are under fourteen, they will get in free.

The garden specialises in plants for specific types of soil and conditions. For instance, there is the Scree Garden planted with alpines and herbaceous Salvias. Then there is the Water Garden containing water loving plants such as the magnificent, enormous Gunnera. This plant has the biggest leaves of any plant that I know, big enough to live in. Iris and Rudbekia are prolific here too. In the Gravel Garden there are plants that are drought tolerant, such as Lavender, Cistus and Bergenias. Finally in the Woodland Garden are plants that like the shade. No matter what type of soil you have in your garden, Beth Chatto will show what you can grow. The trees in the garden are mainly oak and under them in early spring are carpets of Snowdrops and, in September, Cyclamen and Japanese Anemones. The garden is beautiful at all times of the year.

If you get thirsty wandering these lovely gardens, stop in at the Tea House for refreshment or you can take your own picnic and eat it in the grassed area of the car park, they won't mind. Try it, you'll love it.

7

I took the A133 out of Colchester, turned off at Elmstead Market and made for Great Bromley. Here I was looking for Morants Farm, which is the home of Gourmet Mushrooms UK Ltd. run by brothers, Mathew and William Rooney. It was difficult to find, being at the end of a rough track that looks as if it was left behind by the Romans. I arrived on a cold winter morning, parked the car and entered one of a collection of sheds. No one was in. I shouted and knocked loudly on an internal door but got no reply. The lights were on and there was a car parked outside, so I was sure someone was there. Anyway I could not raise anyone. Before giving up however, I went back to my car and sounded the horn. That did the trick; out came Mr Rooney apologising. He was in a far shed, hard at work on his computer and had not heard me knock or call. We settled in his office and had a most interesting chat about mushrooms but it is not worth you making the effort, for you can't buy mushrooms from the brothers direct. You will have to go to Park Fruit Farm of Great Holland or visit one of the farmers' markets at Colchester, Dedham, Barleylands in the county or Stoke Newington, Marylebone, Notting Hill or Islington in London.

Having said that, it is a fascinating place and was an eye-opener for me. Gourmet Mushrooms grow every conceivable mushroom, from cultivated to wild; many of which I had never heard. Names such as Blewits, Hen-in-the-Woods and Nameko. The Rooney brothers gather wild mushrooms from the surrounding woods, and then they use them to develop cultivated ones from them. They reproduce them so providing wonderful, earthy, genuine Essex mushrooms that are perfectly safe to eat. Several wild mushrooms are poisonous and you should never eat them without taking professional advice first. In Spain, most chemists keep lists of poisonous mushrooms and people can take theirs to them for advice. I wish we had such a system in this country, so then we could pick and enjoy some marvellous wild mushrooms without fear. All the mushrooms grown by Gourmet are guaranteed not to kill you. They are all grown naturally on wood, either beech or oak. They are, in fact, one of this country's largest producers of fungi.

Now we know Chestnut, Oyster and even Shiitake mushrooms but they have some which I had never heard of. Such as Enoki – they look like oversized pins, pure white. They are very fine and delicate and require very little cooking. They recommend that you add them to a stir fry or risotto at the last minute. Then there are Shimeji. These are one of Gourmet's top sellers. They have a sweet, creamy nutty flavour and are ideal simply fried in butter or added to a risotto. They come in clusters on their root which you have to discard before cooking, plus a few millimetres of the stems. Finally, Nameko. This mushroom has an earthy, forest flavour which is enhanced when sautéed with shallots and the silky texture withstands the sautéing process well. The layer of naturally occurring gelatine on the cap allows Nameko to thicken soups and sauces. The beautiful, bright orange colour and glossy, moist texture of this mushroom adds an enchanting dimension to culinary creations. It is a wonderful complement for meat, fowl and game. This is what Mr Rooney told me and he's the expert.

There are some very interesting ways you can serve wild mushrooms and Mr Rooney gave me some of his own recipes which he very kindly allowed me to reproduce here for you.

Blewits stewed in milk with sage. Clean the wild Blewits of soil then stew them with chopped onions and a sprig of sage in a little milk over a low heat until soft. Then drain off the milk and thicken it with a little butter and flour and season lightly. Next, pour the resulting sauce over the mushrooms and heat through. Serve in a ring of mashed potato.

White cloud mushrooms with cherry tomatoes and feta cheese. Cut the tomatoes in half, tear the white cloud into similar sized pieces and mix both with the feta cheese. Drizzle over a little olive oil and a squeeze of lemon juice. Sprinkle with fresh parsley or coriander and serve.

Beefsteak mushrooms with hen-in-the-woods risotto. Wash the beefsteak under cold water and slice thinly. Tear the Hen-in-the-Woods into strips, cleaning as you go, (this will take a bit of time, but it is worth it). Heat some chicken or vegetable stock and keep it simmering. Fry some mild onions and garlic in vegetable oil until soft, add mushrooms and cook for five minutes. Add rice and allow the grains to absorb any liquid. Slowly add the hot stock, a few ladles at a time, allowing the rice to absorb the stock each time. When cooked, add some butter and grate parmesan on each serving. Goes well with a spicy salad like ruccola.

I can't wait to try them out. By the way, you will surely have seen those giant white puffball fungi, but did you know that it was edible? I didn't. So, according to Mr Rooney, this is what you can do. Slice the puffball into thick slices, dip into beaten egg and then coat with seasoned flour. Fry the slices until they are lightly browned on both sides.

If you or a member of your family have a gluten or dairy intolerance, head for Great Bromley. At number 11 Meadow Close you will find The Right Cake Company. Annie, who owns and runs the business, explained to me the origins of the company. She discovered that her son was celiac and decided to do something about it. All her products are gluten and dairy free and she has some interesting things. She has won many awards, the most recent being the best new business.

Annie will make any kind of cake you desire, birthday, Christmas, wedding or a cake for any old celebration. Tell her what you want and she will design it, discuss it with you and make it. She will deliver it to you if you live in her area, or you can collect it from her at Great Bromley. She does have some standard cakes, often keeping some in stock. Her favourites are Lemon Drizzle, Chocolate Brownies and perhaps the most interesting of all, Rocky Road. This is a cake with a biscuit base containing plain chocolate and marshmallow. Sounds delicious.

The Right Cake Company shows at Rowhedge farmers' market and you can find them in several garden centres around the county. However, if you are ever near Frinton, go to Le Koffs coffee shop where you could enjoy your favourite. I don't eat a lot of cakes but I am always on the look out for interesting puddings. Why not try the Lemon Drizzle with custard or the Chocolate Brownie with cream. I would.

You simply must not leave Great Bromley without visiting Primrose Pork. You will find their farm shop on Hall Road. When I was there I was delighted to see about 300 beautifully clean pigs all routing about in the surrounding fields. Dotted about the countryside were little huts, that I believe are called Arks. These are the pigs' houses; a far cry from the old fashioned sties. The pigs all appeared to be very happy and it was a great pleasure to see them.

At Primrose Pork you can buy free range pork, both fresh and frozen. They sell their own sausages, sausage meat, pork and apple burgers, chops, joints and, of course, bacon. Somehow meat from a clean, happy pig that is free to wander about at will, tastes so much nicer than the stuff you buy in the average supermarket. I know, for I bought some and can assure you that, once you have tried Primrose pork, you will not want any other.

I bought a boned belly of pork weighing four lb and this is what I did with it.

I broke up about three ounces of crustless white bread and put it in the food processor together with six sprigs of parsley and two ounces of pitted prunes and processed it finely. I then grated a small onion and an apple, peeled and cored and mixed it into the crumb mixture with a tablespoon of lemon juice and salt and pepper. I laid this in the centre of the belly of pork, rolled it up and tied it with string tightly. I sprinkled the skin with salt and roasted it, skin side up at 180c for about two and a half hours. If you have fahrenheit it would be 350f or gas mark four.

After leaving Great Bromley I turned off the A120 and made for Bradfield. Here I found I was passing through fields and fields of soft fruit bushes, so when I spotted a sign announcing D.G.Williamson Ltd, knowing they were fruit growers, I decided to investigate. In about 120 acres Williamsons produce raspberries, strawberries, blackberries, black and red currants, gooseberries and rhubarb. I was able to have a brief chat with Graham, but he was extremely busy and I didn't want to waste his time. In fact the whole farmyard had an atmosphere of hectic activity. They freeze the fruit as soon as it is picked and it is shipped out to retailers and farm shops. In the season, they supply a lot of their fruit fresh, but the frozen fruit is available all the year round. There is no point in you visiting them because they do not sell retail. At least it does show what the fertile soil of Essex can produce.

Did you know that strawberries and rhubarb make good partners? Stew them together with a little sugar syrup or honey, adding a teaspoon of mixed spice. Bake them in a pie.

While I was in the area of Bradfield, I took a look at Mistley nestling quietly alongside the River Stour looking across to Suffolk. Mistley was a medieval village which, sadly does not exist any more. In the 18th century, the local MP had designs on turning the village into a spa town. He began by getting Robert Adam to remodel the parish church, St. Mary the Virgin. He turned it into a most unconventional Georgian church, more like a Palladian mansion. He placed a classical tower at both the north and south ends of the building. These towers are now all that is left of the building. The spa idea did not progress, except for the Swan Basin at the entrance to the village. This is a circular pool which has a life size model of a white swan in the centre. It was intended as the entrance to Mistley Spa. It remains looking lonely and neglected.

The quay, once the scene of great activity was, when I was last there, largely dead. However, Mistley remains one of the curiosities of Essex and is worth taking a look at. Further down river, east from Mistley, you will eventually come to Harwich, well known as the starting point for the ferries to northern Europe. On Harwich Green you will find a most unusual crane. It is a treadmill crane that was in use from 1667 until 1927. It has two big wheels inside a cabin in which two men walked, so winding the gib. I wondered whether the two men inside were convicts condemned to the treadmill as punishment. However, I was assured by the locals that this wasn't so. They were just ordinary dock workers who did the treading in shifts. The crane was removed to its present site in 1932 and has become part of the wonderful tapestry of curiosity of Essex.

One of East Anglia's famous sons is the painter, John Constable. Unfortunately for us we have the misfortune that he was born across the Stour in Suffolk. But fortunately for us, he attended the grammar school in Dedham in Essex, so we can claim to be truly part of Constable Country. Once an opulent wool town in the 15th century, Dedham now is a mecca for tourists from all over the world, not only because of its association with John Constable, but also because of another English artist, Sir Alfred Munnings. Sir Alfred lived in Dedham and his house, Castle House, is open to the public from April to September on Wednesdays, Sundays and bank holiday Mondays. It is crammed full of Munning's paintings and, for art lovers, it is a rare opportunity not to be missed. Another attraction in Dedham is the Dedham Vale Family

Farm. Here you will find many animals ready and willing to play with you.

From Dedham, follow the route of the river and you will come to Stratford St Mary which I call the last village in Essex. Here is the Hall Farm Shop where you will have one last chance of some excellent Essex shopping before landing up in Suffolk. I am tempted to say that John and Stella stock everything that you could possibly want in the way of fresh food. Home reared beef and lamb, home grown potatoes, fresh vegetables and fruit, daily baked bread, free range chickens, duck and quails' eggs, not forgetting local beer, wine and cider. Hall Farm also includes a gift shop and a restaurant.

I was interested in the quails' eggs because you don't see them on sale everywhere. What do you do with quails' eggs? Hard boiled, they sit nicely in a fish pie but what else? How about a Lilliput Breakfast! Fry some slices of bread and cut them into mini triangles. Fry some bacon rashers, then cut them up into small strips. Take some cherry tomatoes, cut them in half and quickly fry them in the bacon fat. Finally, fry some quails' eggs. There you have it, the full English in miniature; fun for the kids.

Turn back towards Colchester and head for Boxted. Carters Vineyard is situated on Green Lane. When I was there, major road works were being carried out and some of the surrounding lanes were closed to traffic. Here in this area you are definitely in the depths of leafy Essex and the signs to Carters are partially obscured by the roadside greenery. However, I eventually found the place but arrived at a most inopportune moment for they were expecting a group of W.I. for lunch and a tasting. The owner, Ben Bunting, realised that I was not a member of the W.I. so showed me around briefly before handing me over to his son Tom, who gave me a more detailed tour of the vineyard. He also showed me a video of the production method and some of the activities they do during the season. One was of particular interest. In the old days, grapes were pressed by foot; pickers trampling on them in large vats. Modern hygiene does not allow this any longer and some say that it is a pity! Anyway, it must have been good fun, so much so that Carters pickers decided to resurrect the old tradition. Not all the grapes are suitable for producing wine, so the discarded ones are placed in a great pot and the pickers dance on them in the old fashioned way. I wasn't sure what happened to the juice so produced, but I didn't dare ask.

Carters produce three white wines, Bacchus, Orion, St Helena, one Rose and two very good reds, King Coel – voted wine of the year in 2006 – and Boudicca. They also do a sparkling Rose and a Brut. They produce Cider, Sloe Gin, Cherry and Plum liqueurs. All this in spite of not being connected to mains electricity or water. They have harnessed nature, using solar panels and a wind turbine to create the power and have a reed filtration bed for their natural water.

Because of the wet weather, I was not able to walk the rows of vines but I was able to reach the lakeside and see a little of the nature trail. Take a break at Carters, see how sunshine is turned into wonderful wines, taste some, wander the nature trail, enjoy the video, all this for a nominal fee.

Boxted is a village that goes back to the 11th century, but not much remains of its early history. One notable feature is the road that runs straight through the area. It's as straight as a Roman road which perhaps it once was, as there is a legend that there was a Roman fort there which was destroyed by Queen Boudicca. The council seems to have run out of ideas when naming their roads, so they called this one simply, Straight Road; it has its namesake in Damascus which is mentioned in the Bible.

Situated half way along Straight Road is McLaughlans, a pick your own establishment. When I arrived at McLaughlans, it was pouring with rain and Mrs McLaughlan's first question was, 'are you intending to pick in this weather?' I assured her that I was not, and in any case it was right at the end of the season, so there would have been precious little fruit left to pick. The best time for you to visit would be between June to mid-August. The farm consists of fourteen and a half acres of fruit and in season they have strawberries, raspberries, gooseberries, black and red currants. I believe they also have some vegetables, such as broad beans and, for good measure, a few sunflowers. It is good fun picking your own fruit but it can be hard work, so if you don't feel like it, you can buy ready picked in the farm shop.

Make a change from the usual redcurrant jelly, mix it with blackcurrant. Take 2 lbs red and 2 lbs black currants, three pints water and 2lbs Sugar. Boil the fruit until it is thoroughly cooked and soft. Strain into a large saucepan, add a teaspoon of mixed spice or, if you are brave enough, a teaspoon of chopped chilli. Add the sugar and boil energetically until it sets when tested. Pour into jars and allow to cool.

You are close to another of Essex's curiosities in nearby Ardleigh. Gnome Magic on Old Ipswich Road. Anathema to a lot of adults but fun for children, are garden gnomes. At Gnome Magic you could read a book while your kids enjoy themselves. Gnome Magic has a lovely garden which leads into a fairy wood. In the wood live hundreds of garden gnomes of all types, shapes and sizes. You could take a wander through the trees and see how many of the creatures you can find. Some are cleverly hidden. If you approach from the A12, leave at Junction 29, take the Old Ipswich Road and you are there.

Tucked away in the countryside beyond Copford Green lies Walnut Tree Farm the home of Linden Lady Chocolates. Before getting back to Colchester, I called on them. For the past twenty-five years they have been making and selling their wonderful handmade chocolates. You may buy them direct by mail order at lindenlady@btconnect.com or you can get them from the Stratford St Mary farm shop, where you will see the full collection. Alternatively, if you are near any Waitrose branch, they stock them. I went in to my local Waitrose and I found a Linden Lady chocolate bar for £1.99, Chocolate Dates and Cherries/Mint Stars at 4.99, Chocolate Fudges at £4.99 and a four-box Chocolate selection at £2.99. Prices do change, so don't take these as gospel.

If you do succumb to temptation, try some grated on to ice cream.

I cannot understand why anyone would leave their home in the lovely island of Antigua and settle in Essex. That's exactly what Cicely did and I am very glad that she did. In Colchester she runs, with only one assistant, Cicely's Cakes and Savouries. She not only will make a gift cake for you for a birthday or wedding but also will sell you her range of regular cakes, such as Victoria Sponge and Rich Fruit and Rum, in four sizes. She has Fruit/Rum Loaf, Ginger Loaf, Chocolate, Carrot, Cheese and Fresh Cream Cakes. All her cakes are laced with the spices of the Caribbean such as cinnamon, nutmeg, ginger and you can really taste the warmth of Antigua in them. Through her cakes, she brings the sunshine of the Caribbean to Essex.

Cicely shows her range at the Colchester and Wivenhoe farmers' markets and in London at Alexandra Palace. You can place an order with her direct on 01206 504723 and collect it yourself and meet the delightful Cicely. Go on, place an order and bring a slice of the Caribbean into your home.

Finally in Colchester, a must is The Colchester Museum housed in the castle on Rygate Road. The town was once the capital of Roman Britain but today, it is not even the county town of Essex. Unfortunately there is not a lot left of the Romans these days but a few artefacts like a coin, a vase, a bronze statue of their God Mercury and a few bits of pots. However, there is a lot left of the Roman wall and its outline can still be traced all around the town.

The Norman castle keep was laid on the foundation platform of the Roman Temple of Claudius, the remains of which can still be seen. The keep itself was the largest ever build in Britain and is one of the largest in Europe. The museum has a fascinating collection of things and traces the history of the town, including its destruction by Queen Boudicca when she slaughtered around 30,000 inhabitants. Since that time, the population has recovered somewhat for it is now around 185,000. Since the 16th century, the castle has been a library and a prison. At one point it was a prison for witches. I don't think there are any witches left now living in the castle, but I bet there might be a few left in the town!

8

Take the B1025 Mersea Road out of Colchester and you will soon arrive at Bourne Mill. This charming old building, sits quietly beside what used to be the stewpond, of St John's Abbey, long since demolished. The stones of the Abbey were used to build the present mill. It was built in 1591 and there seems to be some doubt as to why it was built, especially with its Dutch gable ends. One record says it was built as a fishing lodge and another, an Elizabethan banqueting house. I like to think of it as the latter, a house for pleasure in those playful Elizabethan years. I can picture the scene with serving wenches rushing around with steaming food, consisting of excellent Essex produce. Gentlemen in their finery and ladies in their crinolines, having carefree evenings throwing bones over their shoulders. Be that as it may, fun and games soon came to an end and the building became more serious and was converted to a mill in the early 1800s. The water wheel, which still works, is unusual in that it is inside the building, not outside.

I would suggest you telephone 01206 572422 to check on opening times for they appear to be somewhat erratic. From what I could understand, the mill is open in June from two to five pm, Sundays only and for the months of July and August, from two to five pm Thursday and Sundays. Apart from this it is open on the Sundays and Mondays of bank holidays.

On the B1026, Abberton Road south of Colchester I found Tea Time Cakes For You run by a very enterprising young lady. Some eighteen months ago, Jackie decided to set up her own business making cakes. She makes an interesting range, including sugar, dairy, gluten free cakes. She makes to special order and you can order by phone on 01206 738906 or on line at www.teatimecakesforyou.co.uk and she will post them to you. You cannot collect from her address but you will more than likely find her displaying her standard range at the farmers' markets in Hockley, Stanway and Maldon. She will take orders for birthday cakes, Christmas cakes, wedding cakes and any speciality cake you desire including the fashionable cup cakes. Send her some ideas for a design and leave it to her to come up with something special. Might be worth giving it a whirl.

Before leaving the Colchester area you should pay a visit to Colchester Zoo. It is on the B1026 Maldon road but perhaps the easiest way to it would be to leave the A12 at Eight Ash Green and follow the brown tourist signs. Colchester Zoo is not only a place to see animals, it is a place where there are lots of things to do. You can help feed the elephants and giraffes – that is if you are tall enough – you can visit the 'Wild About Animals Theatre' and play with the creepy-crawlies. You can even be a keeper for a day. See some of the ugly looking reptiles, or the awesome big cats and cute small animals. Watch the antics of the primates and the curious behaviour of the penguins. Did you know what an Aardvark was? I didn't, but I found out at Colchester Zoo. They have over 250 species of animals, some very rare and it really must be one of the best zoos in the world.

Oh by the way, I forgot to ask, did the television stars, the Meercats, come from Colchester? They have plenty of them there. Perhaps someone will tell me.

Situated on the B1026, which is a minor road linking Colchester and Malden is the Abberton Reservoir. The visitor centre is just south of the village of Layer-de-la-Haye and to find it just follow the brown tourist 'wildfowl centre' signs. The reservoir, which is an artificial lake really, covers some 1200 acres and is the largest body of freshwater in Essex. It was created by damming a shallow valley and pumping water from the rivers Chelmer, Blackwater and Stour. During world war two, the reservoir was used to practice the raid on the Mohne Dam in Germany using the famous bouncing bombs. So we can claim that Essex contributed to the success of this raid.

The reservoir has become a wonderful habitat for water birds of every type. There are five hides from which you can watch thousands of different birds, both in the trees and on the water. Many swans and Canada geese make their homes here and sometimes you can see birds that are rarely seen in England. Without a doubt it is one of the finest places for bird watching in the country.

After visiting the Abberton Reservoir, I was making for the B1022 when I passed the Layer Marney Nurseries, calling itself 'Growing Together'; it was in the tiny village of Smythes Green. On an impulse, I went in. I'm glad I did. It was one of the most inspirational nursery gardens that I have ever been in. You enter from a dull little car park behind a shed and are immediately in a lovely garden. It is laid out with a central, round, planted area bordered by alcoves, which are planted up with imaginative displays. It is so peaceful it made me want to study the plants more. If this is what the garden designer intended, he or she has been very successful. Beyond the garden is a farm shop. As well as the various plant, vegetables and herbs, it sells all the gourmet foods that one comes to expect in such shops. Tiptree jams and Marriages flour were two local Essex products I spotted. But it doesn't end there. Growing Together run gardening and garden design courses. So, if you want to learn how to garden properly, give them a ring on 01206 330695.

Now I come to perhaps the most famous firm in Essex, Wilkin & Sons Ltd. Whichever way you approach the town of Tiptree, you will see little brown road signs directing you to the jam museum. Take the B1023 towards Tollesbury on the River Blackwater and you will soon come to the factory of

Wilkin & Sons jam makers, which houses the museum. This company is probably one of the most famous companies in England; certainly it is the leading manufacturer of jams and preserves in the country, if not the world. They have been making jam since 1885 and they now produce over 100 different varieties, thirty-seven conserves, fifteen different marmalades as well as lemon curd, honey and savoury sauces including barbecue and tomato.

Wilkin & Sons have a very friendly face and you will be sure of a warm welcome there; you will not be disappointed. You can browse the shop, which displays hundreds of products, spend hours in the museum inspecting the ancient machinery and finding out what life was like in the 19th century. After that you should settle yourself in the teashop for a well earned cup of Tiptree tea and, of course, jam sandwiches.

There are many hundreds of things that you can do with jam. Get some flour tortillas, spread one side with jam, add some grated cheese to one half of the circle, fold over, seal the edges carefully and bake in the oven or, melt a little butter in a non-stick frying pan and fry them for a few minutes on both sides, which takes about a couple of minutes. Here are some other ideas for you.

Perk up vegetables such as carrots or sweet potatoes with apricot, peach or pineapple jam. Baste ham steaks with strawberry, apricot or cherry jam. Serve roast pork with pineapple, apricot, cherry or peach jam. Serve poultry with cherry, raspberry, peach, apricot or pineapple jam. Serve beef with quince jelly.

Finally one of my favourites originated across the channel. In France there is a town called Bar Le Duc where they specialise in making redcurrant jam. It is ridiculously expensive, for a small pot of say around 30g costs £8.00. Why is it so expensive? The redcurrants are grown locally, almost within a few feet of the town and are picked by hand; no machinery is used here. A group of about twenty to twenty-five women arm themselves with goose quills – yes a feather from a goose – and with them they carefully extract the seeds from each redcurrant. It takes hours. The resulting pulp is turned into Bar-le-Duc confiture. Naturally it is in limited supply and is sold mainly in shops in the town and in only the poshest of French grocers, like Fauchon in Paris.

A dessert was invented for King Louis XIV of France, which consisted of this jam in ice cream. What you do is take small bombe moulds, fill them with ice cream to about two thirds, then spoon out a hole in the middle and fill with the jam. Continue filling the moulds to the top with ice cream. Make sure the jam is completely enclosed. Put them in the freezer. When ready to serve, take the moulds out of the freezer, run hot water over the outsides and de-mould. Seems a lot of work for jam and ice cream to me.

If you want to try it, don't bother with a goose feather, just buy a pot of Tiptree redcurrant jam and carry out the procedure as above. You can of course, use any of Tiptree's excellent jams in this dessert, King Louis won't mind.

If you are in need for some fencing for your paddock, or an electric fence to protect your valuable livestock, go to Hatfield Peveral, a large village just north of Chelmsford. There you will find Upsons Farm Sales, Ivy Barns, The Green, who have everything you will need. Perhaps you don't want to buy eggs, but want some chickens to provide them for you all year round. You can choose the hens – even a rooster – that you fancy. They can also supply all the paraphernalia you will need to keep your chickens happy. If you need to bribe the kids into being quiet while you browse, you can buy them toys and books, all on a country or farm theme. In fact it is quite amazing what a large range of products they have. Oh and we mustn't forget they do sell farm fresh produce from their local area including cheese, frozen foods, ice cream and locally reared meat. A real country store.

When you are driving around the eastern side of the county, look out for bees. They will be buzzing about collecting pollen to produce our wonderful Essex honey. Clive de Bruyn, a gentleman who I would call as busy as a bee, has apiaries all over the county in places like Witham, Tollesbury, Marks Tey and Mersea Island. He is probably one of the biggest producers of hive products in the county. His honey is sold mainly to commercial packers but he does sometimes appear at various farmers' markets in Essex. Honey can be bought in practically every farm shop in the county and, the chances are it will have come from Clive's bees.

Why not warm up a little honey, drop some fruit of your choice in it and coat it well, then serve it with ice cream or even double cream. Drizzle honey over roasted carrots and parsnips and even shallots. A mixture of honey and olive oil is very good for roasting vegetables too.

Making my way back toward Colchester I kept coming across road signs pointing to Layer Marney Tower. They seemed so insistent and after about the third such sign, I decided to follow it. After a short while I came to a simple, unimpressive gateway. It was labelled, Layer Marney Tower. The gate was open, so I drove in and up the driveway. Soon, confronting me was a huge red brick towered gateway. Built in the strict Tudor style, it was very impressive. It was built in the early years of Henry VIII's reign and was intended to be the entrance to a grand courtyard beyond which was to be the actual house. The courtyard and the house were never built. Only two ranges were built, one on each side of the gateway, intended to be the servants' quarters and the stables. The isolated south range to the rear is all there is of the house; it now contains the long gallery. There are several of these red brick gatehouses in East Anglia, but this one is certainly the most impressive. From time to time they hold shows, exhibitions and all sorts of other activities. You can even get married there. Layer Marney Tower is certainly well worth a visit, even if you are not getting married.

The estate also contains a rare breed farm which is home to British Saddleback Pigs, Soay Sheep, Bagot Goats, a herd of Red Deer and Red Poll cattle and many of the animals can be seen in the surrounding fields.

The Food Company at 86 London Road, Marks Tey has to be the most bizarre company that I have ever come across. Their only outlet is squeezed between the thundering A12 and the A120. You can't miss their modern looking store, it is right opposite a Shell garage.

Now why do I call it bizarre? Bizarre is the only word for some of their products. You may well find this hard to believe but to start with they offer Toasted Ants; ants specially bred to be edible, not the sort you scrape up from your garden. Now I have eaten ants and their eggs several times in Mexico. It was a favourite food of the Aztecs but I certainly didn't expect to find them in Essex. Apart from toasted, they have them chocolate covered too. They have ants trapped in a lollipop which they call Ant Lix Lolly, not surprisingly. They also sell delicious Tarantulas which have been oven baked. They have scorpions, presumably baked or even covered in chocolate. I hope they removed their stings, but I suppose you could use them as toothpicks if you're careful. One of their items is a Mint Lollipop which sounds a bit tame, but I expect it has something unusual lurking inside it. They also sell tea but not just ordinary tea; their tea was picked by monkeys. Yes you heard it, monkeys not people. Their coffee comes from beans that have been eaten by a creature called a Civet, a cat-like animal that lives in the forest, and excreted. It is then packed ready for you, if you like. They tell me it is differently delicious and I will take their word for it.

You probably think that I am making all this up, but I assure you that I am not. If you don't believe me, go and find out for yourself. An idea just occurred to me: this stuff sounds perfect for a Halloween party.

Don't let me fool you into believing that edible insects are all that The Food Company sells, far from it. I was shown around by the youthful director, Matt Panks, who introduced me to his many and varied merchandises. I was very impressed because it became apparent that this is a sophisticated store up there with the best of them and quite definitely equals the finest that the west end of London can offer. You name it, The Food Company have got it. On entering the store you are confronted by a splendid display of local fresh fruit and vegetables. Beyond that you will find a chiller cabinet filled with fresh meat and poultry, some of which is already marinated ready to fling into your oven. I bought a pack of venison, which I couldn't wait to cook. The grocery section is extensive from the humble Heinz beans right up to the most exotic tinned products. Their range of spices and curry powders will satisfy the most exacting chef. At the back of the store is the chilled and frozen food area nestling alongside a sparkling display of fresh fish, which was certainly made to be tempting.

I have only just begun, but I can't possibly mention everything. I can only offer an aperitif. Talking of which, the booze section is wondrous. The person who does the buying, certainly knows his business. My host in Essex, who accompanied me to The Food Company, is someone who knows his wines. He told me that he thought that their selection of wine was the best in Essex. Now there's an accolade.

The shop is on two floors and upstairs is a café and the rest of the floor is laid out with housewares. But not ordinary housewares, they certainly have that, but a marvellous collection of funky merchandise too. For instance, cushions large enough for several people to sleep on, a standard lamp in the form of a deferential servant, a chair in the shape of a face mask and, last but by no means least, sparkly crocodiles from very small up to lifesize – but I was assured they don't bite. They'd make a wonderful table decoration for a party.

I could go on but I won't; all I will say is, don't bother to go up to Harrods or Fortnum and Mason, you have it all here in Marks Tey. I was truly excited by The Food Company but it really didn't surprise me for it proves once again that there is more to Essex than meets the eye.

Just down the road from Marks Tey is the village of Stanway, almost a suburb of Colchester. The village has a unique claim to fame. In 1996 archaeologists were called in to investigate some puzzling subterranean enclosures that had been identified from the air. Upon doing a little digging they discovered several graves, one of which was believed to have been that of a druid; thought to have been a doctor of the early Roman period. However, as far as I know, Druidism is no longer practiced in Stanway, but vegetarian cookery is. Leeora's Gourmet Kitchen, in one of the units on Fiveways Fruit Farm on Heath Road, produce vegetarian, vegan and gluten free dishes. They produce wraps, humous, veggie burgers and vegetarian mince, amongst other things. Contact them on 01206 330334 and they will give you details of all their products. You can order by phone or online at order@leeoras.co.uk and they will prepare the food for you.

Back in Marks Tey I found a Candy Man. Julian Pay runs a company called Candy Carnival and he toils away in his kitchen, making fudge. He makes many varieties but he tells me that in Essex, the alcohol flavours sell best. I wonder why? He does not sell from his house but I am sure if you telephoned him and ordered a £100 worth of fudge, he'd be very happy. You will find him at most farmers' markets, including Colchester and at delicatessens and farm shops throughout the county. He has over twenty different flavours and overall, one of the best is Irish Cream but the various alcohol flavoured fudge is by far the best seller.

In and around the village of Aldham there are many food producers. On Rectory Road for instance, I came across Crapes Fruit Farm, owned by a well known local farmer, Mr Andrew Tann. I walked in between farm buildings into the nearest orchard. There was not a soul in sight. All was peaceful and still, except for a family of rabbits chasing each other around the trees, which stretched away into the distance in straight lines. As soon as the rabbits spotted me, they scarpered, obviously fearing they might become the main ingredient of a pie. The area of the orchards is a wildlife habitat with many animals, birds and insects allowed to live unmolested. Insects that devour the aphids and birds in their turn devouring the insects so that the trees are allowed to grow organically without damage and we are able to eat English apples that taste as apples should.

Mr Tann probably grows more apples than anyone else in the country. England has always been famous for its apples and it has angered me that whenever I visit a supermarket, hardly an English apple is to be found. Why do we import apples from France and from as far away as New Zealand, when we have such superb apples in this country? Crapes Fruit Farm grows about 150 varieties of apple over fifteen acres of orchard. You name it, they grow it. Their leaflet not only lists the seventeen top varieties, it also tells you when they are in season.

On the list are some old names I remember from my childhood, such as Beauty of Bath, Laxtons, Worcester Pearmain and Cox's Orange Pippin. Perhaps one of the most interesting of the old varieties is D'Arcy Spice, an apple that had largely disappeared until revived by Andrew Tann. The farm also produces tomatoes, plums, quince and the very rare medlar. This fruit was known to the Romans, but it didn't become popular in Britain until the Victorian period. It has now largely disappeared from the market, except Wilkins do produce a Medlar Jelly, but Mr Tann has the fruit in November.

So how can you get these apples? Well you can go to the farm in person, visit the shop, take what apples you want and put your money through a slot in the wall! Be aware, however that the farm is closed on Sundays. Alternatively you can order by phone on 01206 212375, online at Andrew.tann1@virgin.net and they will send your order by post. For people in their local area, Crapes Fruit Farm does weekly deliveries on Fridays. One thing you should bear in mind, they do not accept credit or debit cards and cash but they will accept a cheque.

If you bought some cooking apples, why not marry them up with cream cheese and make a cream cheese and apple tart? What you do is bake a pastry case blind and, for the filling you will need three cooking apples, peeled, cored and cut in half. Place 4oz sugar, juice of half a lemon and half a pint of water in a saucepan, bring to the boil and reduce it to a syrup. Add the apples and cook until just tender. Remove the apples. Cream 8 oz of cream cheese with 2 oz sugar, spread over the bottom of the pastry case. Arrange the cooked apple halves, cut side down on the cheese. Put two teaspoons of water into a saucepan, add two tablespoons of honey and stir over a low heat and when completely mixed, allow to cool slightly and then pour over the apples. Chill in the fridge until wanted.

After leaving Crapes Fruit Farm, driving along Rectory Road, I spotted a very pretty cottage with a curious name, Half A Loaf Cottage. I stopped and found a van parked in the garden bearing the livery 'The Chocolate Chef'. This was too good to miss, so I knocked on the door. Matt answered my knock; he told me he was not the chocolate Chef but his wife, Cathy was. Unfortunately she was out. Matt explained that, due to the downturn in business, they no longer made a range of chocolates to sell. They now concentrated on chocolate parties. I imagine these are like Tupperware parties with chocolates instead of dishes. So if you want to throw a chocolate party, Cathy's your girl. I do hope that with the expected business upturn, The Chocolate Chef will be in business again soon.

Feeling rather disappointed, I left Half A Loaf Cottage and drove to Halstead Road in Eight Ash Green. I wanted to visit Bullbanks Farm where the BBC recently filmed a Guinness Book of Records attempt at carving the most faces into pumpkins in an hour. The record stood at 50 and after the film, the score stood at 102. It's mind boggling, 102 in an hour; it took me nearly an hour to carve one, and then it wasn't very good!

Anyway, apart from pumpkins, the farm also grows asparagus and sweetcorn. Everything is only available in its season. Asparagus April to June and sweetcorn, August to September. It's such a pity they don't mature at the same time, for they go together very well. In December, guess what they sell, why Christmas trees of course. So if you want to carve a pumpkin lantern or decorate a tree, go to Halstead Road where you can select one for yourself.

For an asparagus and sweetcorn starter, this is what you can do. Par-boil asparagus tips, don't overcook, toss sweetcorn kernels in butter for a few minutes, add the Asparagus and sauté for five minutes. Serve garnished with parmesan shavings. Simple! Between April and June, you will have to use frozen or tinned corn, but in August, September, I am sure most supermarkets will have imported asparagus on sale.

The farmers of Essex seem to be a trusting bunch and, from what I have seen, their customers are an honest lot. After leaving Eight Ash Green I found myself in Brook Road, outside Aldham Hall Farm. Now don't expect a stately home, it doesn't exist, or at least I didn't see it. What I did see was a collection of barns of an obviously working farm. Aldham Hall is the home of Becketts Potatoes; and inside one of the barns was Mr Beckett. He was sorting potatoes that were rolling down a conveyor belt. I asked him if he sold retail and he directed me to his shop in a shed alongside the barn.

Inside the shed were bags of potatoes, grown on the farm, baskets of vegetables including broccoli, cress, spring onions, celery, carrots, cauliflowers and cabbages, all locally grown. Pre-bagged fruits were on shelves, as were jars of honey and boxes of eggs – all local produce. Everything was marked with its price and, in a prominent place on a shelf, was a box in which to put your money. I suppose what we would call an honesty box. I asked Mr Beckett if he ever lost anything to shoplifters. He didn't think so, for the few times he had bothered to do a tally of what was missing from the shop against money in the box, it was always right and sometimes there was even a little more. From what I saw of the display, it couldn't have been fresher. Straight out of the ground and on to the shelves. Also, I believe that such trust in one's fellow man deserves rewarding.

What I like to do with new potatoes is slice them, fry them lightly, sauté some chopped onion, beat some eggs and pour over the potatoes and onion. I put some cheese on the top and brown under the grill. Another thing I like to do with old potatoes is boil them with garlic cloves. Then I mash with crème fraiche and butter. Then I add some grated or shaved raw carrot.

9

Essex has always been fascinated by railways; before Dr Beeching closed many lines down, Essex had lots of them. There are still more in our county than most other counties in England. There are four passenger-carrying private railways in Essex, as well as five miniature railways and many other disused ones. The one I visited first was the East Anglian Railway and Museum. If you are a railway buff, this is the place for you. It is situated at Chappel/Wakes Colne Station, which is on the A1124, Halstead Road. To get there, leave the A12 at Eight Ash Green. Here you will find everything connected with railways, both steam and diesel. It is a very good museum with plenty of things to interest both you and your children. They run what they call Railway Experience Courses. I'm not sure what these consist of but perhaps they will teach you to drive a train. Certainly you can take train rides. Apart from the museum, they also have a shop, where you can buy model railway items, books and Thomas the Tank Engine merchandise. You can even hire the place for a party. The museum is open every day from 10.00 until 16.30.

In many farm shops throughout the county I found crisps on sale. Not surprising you might say, but what was surprising to me was that they were Essex crisps and I just had to find out about them. From Wakes Colne, I made my way up country to Wormingford. This is on the B1508 the Colchester to Sudbury road but be careful, you're in danger of falling into Suffolk! Fairfields Farm Crisps is on Fordham Road, Wormingford. I really believe that Robert and Laura are two of the bravest farmers in Essex. They grow acres of potatoes and, with them they have entered one of the most competitive markets in the country, crisps. I must say that even though they are competing with the giants of the crisp market, they have more than held their own.

Their potatoes are grown on the farm in Wormingford, shipped to a factory in London, where they are cooked to Fairfield's exclusive recipes and then returned to Essex for packaging and distribution. They have six very tasty varieties; Farmhouse Cheese and Chive, Sweet Thai Chilli, Sea Salt and Cider Vinegar, Ever So Lightly Sea Salted, Smoky Bacon and Sunday Roast Potato and finally, Parsnip and Essex Honey. Now if they don't get your taste buds bouncing, nothing will. Unfortunately you cannot buy from them direct, so there's no point in you climbing up to Wormingford, but you can buy them in practically every farm shop in Essex as well as some of our farmers' markets. You will not find them in any supermarket. If you happen to be catching a train north from Euston Station in London or wanting to take a book out of the British Library, both places sell them. You should try them, I have, they're good.

Sometimes I make up a crispy mash. Boil potatoes normally and mash them. Then smash up a packet of crisps to smithereens and stir them into the mash. You'll be surprised how good it is. You can use any flavour, but if you use sea salt and vinegar or lightly salted, don't add more salt. Another thing I do is make a crispy omelette. Beat up the eggs, add crushed crisps and cook. I find Smoky Bacon and Roast Potato is the best one for this.

I carried on up the B1508 until I came to Mount Bures. After I had crossed the railway line, I turned left into Hall Road and there was Farmer Browns, run by Steve and Heather Brown. This charming little shop is full of wonderful home baked pies, cakes, pasties, quiches and sausage rolls. As soon as I walked in, the smell of baking assailed my nostrils delightfully. I really was excited to find that Farmer Brown is one of the very few bakers who still makes the old fashioned bread pudding, so beloved of our mothers. Made from stale bread, I remember it well as my mother made it during world war two. I ate a piece there and then in the shop and it left me feeling replete and gave me a surge of energy that I needed.

Farmer Brown sells at farmers' markets and you will find their products in most good farm shops. And another thing, if you have to give a dinner party but don't want to cook it yourself, invite Farmer Brown in and he will do all the catering. Yes, there is an actual Farmer Brown but I can't guarantee that he will do the cooking himself.

Another of Farmer Brown's products is cold pressed rapeseed oil. This is a good alternative to olive oil. Now we have all seen those brilliantly glowing yellow fields all over the country. At one point they were all over the place and I began to think that the farmers had over-raped themselves. The seeds of this plant provide an excellent oil that contains half the saturated fat of olive oil, is high in unsaturated fat and contains no trans fats. Of course there are many things you can do with this oil, but if you use it to roast potatoes, you'll be surprised at the difference. If you fancy your potatoes a little more exotic, heat four tablespoons of rapeseed oil, when hot, add a quarter teaspoon of mustard seeds, then add a quarter teaspoon chilli powder and turmeric and fry for one minute. Add your potatoes, which you have boiled and cut into chunks. Make sure they are well coated and fry until they begin to turn brown. Try using rapeseed oil for making mayonnaise and salad dressings or you can go and visit Farmer Brown and he may be able to give you other ideas.

If you happen to be driving on the A131, stop off at the charming old village of Wickham St Paul and call into Spencers Farm Shop. Here you will find a great range of fresh farm produce. Soft fruits, vegetables and pumpkins in season. They also have a pick your own area for fruit and vegetables. When you have finished shopping or picking, call into the farm coffee shop for a welcome cuppa.

One of their innovations is 'table top strawberries'. These are strawberries in the pick your own area that are grown at waist height. Saves all that back breaking bending down! Another of their specialities is the lovely courgette. I love these little marrows and I like to cook them this way: Grate them roughly using the largest section of your grater. Then grate an onion finely. Mix the two together and gently sauté them in butter. You can always add a little spice of your choice; try nutmeg.

After Wickham St Paul get on to the B1058, turn left and after a few miles you will come to a sign to Gestingthorpe on your right. No, I had not heard of Gestingthorpe either. As you approach the village, you will come to a pub/restaurant on the right called the Pheasant. This is the home of Borley Smokery. Leave your car in the little car park and go inside. It will be worthwhile.

When I got there the place was shut. Having driven all that way, I wasn't going to be thwarted. Undaunted, I rang the bell and James, the owner appeared. The place had just been completely refurbished, so no products were on display. But he was able to find something in the fridge for me to buy. James explained that normally there would have been a selection of home smoked items in a cabinet in the bar. The smoked products include salmon, halibut, haddock, scallops, herrings, mackerel, trout, olives, cheese, nuts, chocolate, marmalade, olive oil and prawns. However, they are not all available at the same time, it depends on what James smokes that day. All his products are sourced locally except the salmon which comes from Scotland. I had never heard of smoked chocolate or marmalade and was disappointed that I was unable to taste them. James assured me that they were both delicious. He likes smoking unusual things and, as he keeps bees, he is going to try to smoke honey. I can't wait to try it.

James is a man of many talents and, as well as being a publican, a restaurateur and smoker, he is also a garden designer. Behind the pub is his garden, which won a prize at a recent Chelsea Flower Show.

Do take the trouble to find Borley Smokery and while you are selecting your smokeries, you can sink a pint of local ale. I bought some smoked haddock and this is what I did with it. I put it in a pan with a knob of butter and covered it with milk. I heated it gently, not allowing it to boil, simmered it until it was cooked but still firm. I removed it from the milk. I put a level teaspoon of cornflour in a little of the milk and mixed it in to a thin paste. I then poured it into the rest of the milk, chopped up some fresh parsley, added that and brought it slowly to the boil. I stirred until the sauce thickened. I served it over the haddock with some new potatoes. I also bought some smoked cheese, which I ate with my favourite chutney for a light lunch. Had I been able to buy some smoked mackerel fillets, I would have served them with horseradish sauce.

Incidentally Borley Smokery gets its name from the village of Borley, some three miles away. This is where there was a rectory that was reputed to be the most haunted house in Britain. The story goes that the rectory was built on the site of a Benedictine monastery, which was built in 1362. Legend has it that a nun from nearby Bures Convent fell in love with one of the Benedictine monks and they decided to elope. A friend was to drive them away at night. The elders of the monastery discovered the plan and captured the couple. The coachman was beheaded for his part in the plan, the monk was hanged and the nun was bricked up alive, in the walls of the vaults beneath the monastery which still survive under the site of the old rectory. Their ghosts have haunted the site ever since.

While you are in the northern reaches of the county and you feel like getting married, make for Great Yeldham and stop off at Spencers. This mid 18th century mansion will arrange everything for you. It will provide you with a fairytale setting for your ceremony in the garden among the gorgeous blooms and a marquee in which to dance and dine. Spencers does the lot, marquee, catering, band, flowers and even the priest or registrar, if you prefer. The only thing they will definitely not supply is the bride.

I do recommend that you provide the wedding cake yourself, that way you can have one to your own design. You have a wide choice of cake makers here in Essex. Home Fayre Basildon, Tea Time Cakes Colchester, Ravens of Ingatestone and The Right Cake Company Great Bromley.

At Great Yeldham you will find Tilbury Meadows Pedigree Beef on Hall Farm. This company have a registered pedigree herd of Herefords that graze the Colne Valley flood meadows. This produces meat of premium quality. Some chefs say that it is the best beef you can buy. They sell boxes of beef weighing up to 50 lbs or, if that is too much, they will sell you a half box. A box will contain roasting joints, pot roasts, steaks, stewing steak and mince. Phone them on 01787 237249 or contact them online at beef@jazzfarmer.com and place your order. You won't regret it.

I have my own version of Beef Wellington. This is what I do. I take a 1 lb beef fillet in one piece and sear it on all sides in a frying pan. Leave it to cool a little. Chop up a large plate mushroom into chunks. Chop up an onion and fry until it is what they call translucent. Add the mushroom pieces and cook for a few minutes. Add a tablespoon of brandy and cook till evaporated. Mix in one tablespoon of double cream, mix well. Roll out puff pastry, not too thin, to fit the beef. Cut a piece to form a separate lid. Lay the pastry on a greased baking sheet and put the mushroom/onion mixture in the centre and put the beef on top. Pull up the pastry on all four sides to the top; dampen the edges and place the pastry lid on top. Using the tines of a fork, press the edges down well. Brush all over with beaten egg or milk, to glaze. I bake it for about forty minutes in my fan assisted oven at 170c. A normal oven would be 400f, 200c or gas 6.

While you are in the Colne Valley, you must visit the Colne Valley Railway. You will find them on Yeldham Road, Castle Hedingham. The whole area is a wonderland, especially for children, but if you are a steam train buff, for you too. They have special steam and diesel operating days but it is better to contact them in advance, for they don't operate every day. For the children, there is Thomas the Tank Engine and they can spend the day with him. The miniature railway operates every day. During the year they hold special events and at Christmas there are special 'Days out with Santa'.

Essex is so full of many wonderful places to visit; you'll never be at a loss of what to do with the children during half term or summer holidays. Why bother to go to the expense of the Costa Brava?

Also in the area is Castle Hedingham. This must be one of Essex's most valuable tourist attractions. Just over the border, Suffolk must be green with envy that it isn't in their county. The gigantic Norman keep is all that is left of a medieval castle, but there is plenty more. The castle and grounds are open from April to October and provide a wonderful place to spend the day.

The castle keep is available to hire for weddings. For a few thousand pounds, you can hire the place and they will provide all you need for your wedding; champagne, wedding breakfast and disco. To get the bride there, they can even provide a beautiful Rolls Royce Silver Cloud. You can even rent a cottage in the grounds or the lodge at the gate, just in case your guests can't make it home.

Various exciting events take place during the summer, such as medieval jousting tournaments, super car and classic car displays, teddy bears' picnics, candlelit tours of the ghostly dungeons, classical music concerts and even visits from Shakespeare's Globe Theatre touring company. There is something for everyone, so don't miss it.

If after visiting Castle Hedingham, you fancy some fruit, you could do worse than go to Wash Farm in Queen Street, Sible Hedingham nearby. Provided you go at the right season, you can pick your own to your heart's content. In late April until late June you can cut as much asparagus as you like. In mid June to early August, strawberries are aplenty and raspberries from early July to August. If gooseberries and blackcurrants are among your favourites, go in late June to mid July. If you are wandering about later in the year, say September to October, you will find loads of sweetcorn cobs just waiting for you. However, if you are feeling too lazy to do the picking, they will do it for you. The farm shop is loaded with the stuff but do choose your seasons carefully.

A good thing to do with the fruit you've bought is the traditional Summer Pudding. Gently simmer the fruit of your choice in a mixture of water and honey. Grease a good old fashioned pudding basin with butter and line it with slices of white bread, making sure the sides of the basin are covered. Add your stewed fruit and place more bread on top. Put a layer of foil over the top and place a heavy weight on the top. Leave it in the fridge overnight, or until you want to serve it. Turn out and eat with a dollop of fresh cream. But, if it's gooseberries you bought, make a fool out of 'em.

Driving along the A1124 between Halstead and Earls Colne, I noticed a sign which read Greenstead Farm Shop. This was one I had not heard of, so decided to investigate and I am very glad I did. I followed several little signs to 'farm shop' tucked into the hedgerows along the lanes until I came to the tiny village of Greenstead Green. I turned into a sort of courtyard and there, housed in a beautifully restored 17th century barn was the farm shop.

Inside was a revelation; it had a wonderful display of variety. Fresh and frozen foods, bakery, butchery, grocery, a post office – which included a bureau de change – and a café serving freshly cooked foods from 'Gilberts Galloping Chef.'

In fact the place was a cross between Fortnum & Mason and the village store.

It is very difficult to list the shop's stock because it is so extensive; too extensive for a village store, I thought. I questioned the manager Daphne who explained that, since opening four years ago, their reputation had spread far and wide. They did no advertising; their pulling power was simply by word of mouth. Their pastries, fresh every day from the Gilbert Galloping Chef outfit, included pasties, quiches and sausage rolls. The deli section was extremely sophisticated and their cheeses included such rarities as the Welsh Black Bomber – which I can't even find in London. Their range of herbs and spices left nothing to be desired and, of course, they had a wonderful range of local fruit and vegetables. Daphne told me that she sourced as much as she could from the local area, which was borne out by the range of Essex favourites on display, such as Hadleys, Farmer Bills, Priors Hall, Wicks Manor and Tiptree. The barn also included a gift shop, showing a lot of ceramics, a toy shop to the delight of many kids, a kitchen shop geared to the most discerning chef and an art gallery showing works from local artists.

On the other side of the courtyard, housed in another converted barn, was a shop selling feed for cattle, pigs, dogs, cats and even rabbits. They also stocked a wide range of country clothing, riding tackle, cleaning materials and horse blankets. They were a separate company from the Greenstead Farm Shop, but they worked in tandem. I found the whole of my visit fascinating and you will too.

Right in the middle of the High Street in Earls Colne I found Margaret's Frozen Luxuries. Now here is a truly Essex company even though the product is no longer made in Essex. This is because of its success and their kitchen can no longer cope with the demand. Their product is frozen yoghurt which is a very healthy alternative to ice cream. If anything can be said to have the wow factor, this frozen yoghurt certainly has it. It comes in four flavours, mango, raspberry, strawberry and natural lemon. Until recently it only came in 120ml tubs (with spoon attached to the lid) but now, due to customer demand, they sell it in 500ml tubs as well.

Margaret Salmon and Paul Brown are a delightful couple who are very enthusiastic about their product. They insisted I tried it and I didn't need much persuading. As I tucked into a tub of strawberry, they were not going to be left out, so had a tub each themselves. Now that's dedication for you. No greater proof of a product is required than when the maker can't resist eating it themselves. They do not do farm gate sales but you could order online at: www.margaretsfrozenluxuries.co.uk Most of their sales are to local farm shops and delis. Wholesale is handled by the Tastes of Anglia organisation and they handle all deliveries.

Both Margaret and Paul have a farming background and searched the country for the right quality milk and cream for their yoghurt. They finally settled on the Channel Islands for their milk. Their fruit is from Essex, except of course mango and lemon which they import. They sell their product at county shows, piling into their liveried van, setting up their stand and making it right on site. They even dress for the part, both in matching shirts and hats and very colourful they look. It was very obvious to me that they both love their product and you will too.

You could make the yoghurt even more luxurious by serving mango with slices of mango and the strawberry and raspberry with the relevant fruit. However, with the lemon I suggest you slice a lemon, halve the slices and poach them in water and a lot of sugar, keeping the rind on. When very syrupy, let them get cold and serve with the natural lemon variety.

Also in this neck of the woods is one of this country's largest and most famous companies, CCL Food Plc, otherwise known as Baxters, makers of fine soups. Their range is extensive and needs no illustration here. I mention the company merely to show that Essex and Essex people are a vibrant, go-ahead lot and we have some excellent, internationally famous companies right here in the county.

Here's a couple of ideas for you to make a little difference. In the summer, serve the soup cold. Take a tin of Baxters Beef Consomme, add some powdered gelatine – the packet will tell you how much liquid to use – heat it slowly, not allowing it to boil, until the gelatine has dissolved. Pour into little individual bowls, place them in the fridge until set. Or, take a tin of Lobster Bisque and serve it like the French Soupe de Poisson. Toast small slices of French bread, rub them with a cut clove of garlic, put some Rouille sauce on them and serve with the soup. You can buy Rouille sauce in any good grocers.

In a rural backwater, just outside the pretty village of Colne Engaine is situated a somewhat unusual farm. Not derelict but deserted, or at least it was when I visited. I found myself in a farmyard in which was a farmhouse and several wooden buildings, one of which was labelled 'shop'. Just inside the door was a table on which was what I call an honesty box. Against one wall was a large, glass fronted freezer cabinet containing samples of the entire range of Hadleys Dairy Ice Cream. There was a bell push on the wall, which promised help. I pushed the button several times without getting any response. I assumed it wasn't working, but nevertheless pushed harder and all I got for my effort was a bruised thumb. I tried telephoning but was referred to a mobile phone number. I tried this and got 'voicemail'. All I could do was rummage through the freezer cabinet, select an ice cream, put my money in the box and leave.

I can tell you nothing about the manufacture of this ice cream, but what I can tell you is the range. There was Rumsoaked Raisin, Baileys, Raspberries and Cream, Vanilla, and finally Elderflower Cream. In the same cabinet there was another range called Farmer Bills which included such flavours as Terrific Toffee, Chunky Chocolate, Vanilla Dream, Double Fudge Delight, Honeycomb Crunch, Mint Choc Chip, Real Strawberry Swirl, White Choc Chunk and Marshmallow Munch. They all sound very interesting. They were available in pots of 950ml and 120ml. I purchased a Terrific Toffee, it was very nice but in the absence of anyone to tell me where the milk came from, whether it was a totally Essex product, it lost some of its excitement somehow. I would have liked to have bought more but it was a very hot day and my car does not have a fridge. I was obviously just unlucky and I am sure you will have better luck. However if you can't get to Hadleys, I have seen it on sale in several farm shops and from what I tasted, it would be well worth your while seeking it out.

E.E.Ullph & Co. Ltd. on Whites Farm, Bures Road, While Colne is where Angus Scobie grows 100 acres of apples. Most of his apples are turned into juice but should you take the trouble to stop by, he will sell you some apples straight off the tree, in the season of course. He might even sell you a jug of juice, but I'm not sure. I tried a couple of bottles and I can tell you it is excellent.

There is another side of Whites Farm and that is swimming! They have converted one of their barns into an indoor swimming pool. This is available for hire by individuals or private parties of a maximum of eight people. It is hired on a contract basis of a half hour slot per week for thirteen weeks. This gives you the private use of the heated pool uninterrupted. There is no life guard but as the pool is only 4'1" deep, one is not necessary. It is much in demand, so if you want your own private swimming pool, contact Angus right away.

On my way back along the A1124 towards Colchester, at Wakes Colne I passed the Wakes Colne Forge. I stopped to have a look around. They make all things in iron, including gazebos, gates, benches, fencing, tables and chairs. However, I was disappointed to find that they were not farriers. They shoed no horses. I admit I was hoping to find a traditional blacksmith with hammer and anvil turning out horseshoes but it was not to be. Anyway, if you are in need of garden furniture or fireside ironwork, Wakes Colne Forge is the place to go.

The area around Coggleshall has more interesting places than almost any other area of Essex. First, in the village itself, is Paycockes, a 16th century merchant's house and nearby are Cressing Temple, Coggleshall Grange Barns and Marks Hall Arboretum as well as some good farms and farm shops. One of the best farms, in my opinion, is to be found on America Road, which is off the B1024, Earls Colne to Coggleshall road.

America Farm is run single-handedly by ex-banker Barry Hadden. He produces Longhorn, Hereford and Highland beef. You can buy from the farm gate, but you must order at least one quarter of the animal. This will consist of half of the fore quarter and half of the hind quarter. This will give you sirloin, rump, fillet, mince, stewing steak, ribs and twelve roasting joints. Barry is very keen on animal welfare and this becomes obvious when you look at his beasts. They all are clean, contented and appear to have very happy faces. Barry says that a happy animal produces better meat. How he manages to run the farm and look after the animals on his own I shall never know, but one thing I am certain of is that no beef could possibly taste better. The slaughterhouse that Barry uses is only twelve miles away and he sends his animals there the day before they are to be slaughtered so that they can settle in and remain unstressed. All this, he assured me, is very important for the resultant quality of the meat. One impression I came away with was that Barry Hadden knows what he is doing.

Beef cooked on the bone is best as the bone acts as a conductor of heat and provides extra flavour. Fat on the meat is important too, for meat without fat will not taste as good as that with fat. Barry recommended shaking a little flour on the meat with some sea salt. He said cook a sirloin joint at 475F, 240C, Gas 9 for the first twenty minutes, then turn heat down to 375F, 190C, Gas 5 for fifteen minutes a pound for rare, plus fifteen minutes for medium and thirty minutes for well done. For a really luxury roast, when cooked take the joint out to rest. Pour Baxters beef consommé mixed with a little cornflour into the roasting tin and stir, scraping up any bits.

The little village of Chappel lies just south of the A1124 at Wakes Colne. When I got there the road into Chappel was closed due to major road works and access to the village was impossible. The only way to get to it was via the A120 through the villages of Great and Little Tey. There are two meat producers in the village, the first one I came to was Direct Meats at Knights Farm who describe themselves as trade butchers. They have very high quality beef and pork which is all sourced locally. They also have a range of chickens and ducks which are sourced outside the county, as well as a huge range of cheeses. They do not supply retail, but you can visit their retail shop, Holts in Witham. Mainly they supply Michelin star restaurants, the Savoy and Claridges hotels in London, as well as, surprisingly, Heathrow airport. I bet you can only get their beef if you are flying first class! They also have a butchery training school, so if you have a son or daughter who wants to become a butcher, sign them up at Direct Meats.

The other company in Chappel is G&J Barron at Puttocks Farm. I had a long and very pleasant conversation with young Ross Barron, who gave me the low down on the company; he even made me a cup of coffee. The business was originally started by his grandfather sixty-five years ago specialising in turkeys, chickens and ducks. They buy their Kellys Bronze turkey chicks when they are a day old and rear them for six months, when they are ready for the table. In the season they will have up to 2000 turkeys, 700 of which are sold at the farm gate. The rest go to farm shops, farmers' markets and local butchers. They do a large trade in corporate sales, supplying banquets and receptions where outside catering is required. Their poultry is available all the year round, but out of the Christmas season, they are frozen. They also do a locally produced range of beef and pork, sausages, bacon, smoked salmon and free range eggs and pheasants from a local shoot. To complete the festive season, they even have Christmas puddings. So if you go there, which I would recommend you to, you can stock up your freezer.

You can order on 01206 210383 or online at orders@barronfarms.co.uk when you can pay by card and they will deliver to anywhere in the United Kingdom.

I bought a duck and this is what I did with it. I dipped it in boiling water for ten seconds, patted it dry, then pricked the skin all over and rubbed it with half a lemon. I ground some sea salt in a pestle and mortar and rubbed it well into the skin. In a little duck fat – if you haven't got any, use olive oil – I put about 200g of black pitted olives, two cloves of garlic, chopped fine and some Thyme leaves. I then added some stale white bread broken into chunks and fried the lot until the bread was golden. I stuffed the duck with this mixture and roasted it. Ross recommended to roast any poultry on high for the first twenty minutes and at a lower temperature for the remainder of the cooking time.

G&J Barron is an excellent, family run farm that has a large, loyal customer base and if you are in the area, you really should call in. You can be sure of a great welcome.

Follow the B1024 toward Coggleshall and turn off when you see the sign to Marks Hall Arboretum. Here you will find lots to delight you. Trees from all over the world have been planted here, many of which I had never heard. One of their latest acquisitions and one of which they are proud to have is the Wollemi Pine. The ancestor of this tree was growing while the dinosaurs were roaming around, probably scratching their backs on its trunk. This tree's family is over 200 million years old. It was thought to have been long extinct until one day, an

Australian wildlife park official discovered it growing in the wilds of New South Wales. Since then it has been widely propagated and samples are now all over the world. The remote area where it was found is a closely guarded secret and is rigidly protected. Just imagine yourself standing under a tree that was being nibbled by a Tyrannosaurus Rex, with a Pterodactyl nesting in its top branches.

The gardens are laid out with thousands of beautiful plants and shrubs and there are many things of particular interest. The Honeywood oak tree, planted over 800 years ago and still standing, is one. Another is the swamp area based on the Florida Everglades; I don't think they have alligators though. The lakes were dug originally by Oliver Cromwell's army in an idle moment during the siege of Colchester. The visitor centre is in a 15th century barn, where you can take refreshments or there's the 18th century coach house where you can get married. If you do decide to visit, a good time to go would be in September when you will see the glorious colours of autumn foliage rivalling those of New England.

Before continuing on to Coggleshall itself, stop off at Blackwells; watch out for the sign to Herons Farm. This is a family run business started by the present owner's grandfather thirty years ago. For many years they concentrated on producing geese and turkeys for the Christmas market but in 2004 they set up The Rare Breed Meat Company to supply leading butchers and food halls with high quality, locally produced pork, beef and lamb. In 2008 they opened their farm shop to sell not only their meat but also fresh vegetables, goats' milk and cheese, wine, beer, honey and preserves. All their produce is locally sourced and an excellent display it is and well worth a visit.

Animal welfare is very important to them and their geese, chickens and turkeys wander freely throughout the fields. Their beef is from long and short horn cattle and they buy beef in Sussex and Hereford beef from a farm in South Devon. The lamb they sell is their local Colne Valley lamb as well as the famous salt marsh lamb from Romney Marsh in Kent. Everything is butchered on the premises by their resident butcher, Roy. Their pork is, of course, Gloucester Old Spot and Blythburgh bred on the north Suffolk coast. All their suppliers have to meet the Rare Breed Company's exacting standards in animal welfare. It must be additive free and reared absolutely in the traditional way.

Where can you buy this meat? Well, in the farm shop at Herons Farm and also in the food halls of Harvey Nichols and Harrods in London as well as top class butchers in Essex and throughout East Anglia. I bought a goose and this is what I did. I turned some stale bread in breadcrumbs and soaked them in Ruby Port. I sautéed some minced onion in butter until translucent. I then added Maldon sea salt and freshly ground black pepper. I took the pan off the heat and added some chopped, dried prunes and apricots. All this mixture went into the goose and I roasted it in the normal way. When it was cooked, I let it rest for thirty minutes. Meantime, I poured off most of the fat from the roasting tin, reserving it to use some other time. I then stirred in some Ruby Port, a chicken stock cube and the water that I had boiled the vegetables in. I scraped up any bits from the pan, brought it to the boil, added a teaspoon of soy sauce and boiled it down to serve with the goose.

No one can pass through the village of Coggleshall without stopping to look at Paycockes. This house was built in 1500 for wool merchant, Thomas Paycocke. It is a clear example of the wealth created by the wool trade in Essex. The amazing half-timbered exterior of the house is truly matched by some stunning carved woodwork and panelling of the interior. Step back in time as you stroll around this unique house before stepping out into the beautiful cottage garden.

Owned by the National Trust, the house is open from the 5th to 27th March, Saturdays and Sundays from 13.00 to 17.00.

From 1st April to 30th October it is open on Wednesday to Sunday 11.00 to 17.00. If you care to combine your visit with that of the Coggleshall Grange Barn, a combined ticket will save you about £1.70 on the entrance fees.

Tucked away just off the main street in Coggleshall is Grange Hill. On Grange Hill is the Coggleshall Grange Barn. This beautiful building has a secret. No one is exactly sure when it was built. Coggleshall Abbey was founded in 1140 by King Stephen and Queen Matilda and the barn may have been in existence then. In 1976 carbon fourteen testing of the oak arcade posts gave a date of 1130. However, in 1994, tree ring analysis came up with a date of construction of between 1237 and 1270. Unfortunately the abbey was dissolved by Henry VIII in 1538 and no records now exist. In any case, whether it was constructed in the 12th or 13th centuries, it is still very old and well worth a visit.

Almost opposite the Grange Barn, down Abbey Lane, I came to Abbey Farm. It's flattering to call it a lane, it was more like a dirt track. Cattle were wandering about the fields, including a small white pony that seemed very interested in me, more for what I could give him than why I was there. Antony Brew, the farmer/owner soon appeared to find out what I wanted. I reminded him of a telephone conversation we had a few days previously. He immediately brightened and couldn't have been more hospitable. He led me into his small house where I was greeted boisterously by his two dogs. Antony described himself as a typical Essex boy, making a living farming the Essex soil and very much into organics. He is a good looking man, and I got the strong impression that there was more to him than farmer but he assured me that he was a true farmer, growing all his vegetables from seed.

Courgettes, chillies, French beans, asparagus are just some of the things he grows. From these he makes chutneys and pickles. He gave me a pot each of Hot Chilli Chutney and Crunchy Courgette Pickle, both made in his kitchen and very deliciously spicy they were. He introduced me to packets of seeds that he had recently acquired from Italy. They were Cavolo Lacinapto and Cavolo Nero. They are a form of kale and come from Tuscany. He intends to sow them in the autumn, when he will be the only farmer in this country producing these little known Italian vegetables. I intend to go back to Abbey Farm and find out how he's doing.

Antony describes his farm as a family smallholding. He is very much a one man band – no pun intended, for he is a musician and a DJ by night – so my first impressions of him were correct. He does not sell retail but I am sure if you turn up you might be able to persuade him to sell you a pot or two. He did sell me a couple of bunches of his asparagus, which is one of his major crops. He supplies local outlets, the local Coggleshall butcher and some of the Co-Op supermarkets. He also supplies to delicatessens throughout Essex.

To me Antony's farm was a rural idyll and I will certainly be going back. I strongly recommend that you look for the simple black and white Abbey Farm label next time you are shopping in Essex. By the way, his chilli chutney is perfect with poached salmon or any fish and you could cut a thick slice of farmhouse bread, lay a slab of your favourite cheese on it, cover with the Courgette Pickle and wash it down with a glass of beer. Some ploughman!

Cut across the fields and make for the village of Feering. Here is Feeringbury Manor. This is a very pretty 14th century house, surrounded by a delightful garden. The house is not open to the public, but the garden is and is well worth a visit. It is filled with flowers, and at all times of the year there are many interesting plants to be seen. The garden is open from May to July and in September on Thursdays and Fridays from 9.00am to 4.00pm.

From Feering take the A12 to Witham, then turn up the B1018 to Cressing Temple, a medieval manor of the Knights

Templar. The estate was granted by Queen Matilda in 1137 to the knights who couldn't make up their minds whether they were monks or soldiers. The two great barns that we see today were built in the 13th century and remain much as they were. In fact, they are reckoned to be the oldest barns in the world. The only other thing that survives from this period is the well, which was dug by the knights' own hands.

There are plenty of things to see and do on the estate. There is the Tudor walled garden, which contains a reconstructed Elizabethan knot garden, a 17th century granary building and a typical moated Essex farmhouse, built in 1603 but remodelled in the 18th century. Various events take place throughout the year such as The Essex Food Show, Antique and Collectors' Fair and Art and Design Fair, to name but a few. There are many more special event days, especially for children.

Cressing Temple is open from April to September from 10am to 5pm and in March and October, from 10am to 4pm. It is also available for conferences and weddings. If you do visit, you can't take your dog with you, but please don't leave him in the car, especially on warm summer days. Leave him sleeping at home, he'll be quite happy. To get more information call 01376 584903/585046 or online at www.cressingtemple.org.uk

Carry on up the B1018 and you will come to Cressing Park Farm Shop. I am not sure if I should say don't take the children with you or not. This farm shop is a paradise for kids and possibly a nightmare for their dentist. On shelves behind the counter are dozens and dozens of glass jars filled with every kind of sweet you can think of, and some that you can't. In fact there are 120 varieties, some old fashioned, like Humbugs, Sherbet Tips, Liquorice Comforts and many more modern ones.

Apart from this, the farm breeds its own pork, lamb and beef and grows all its own fruit and vegetables, all of which are on display. They also stock some interesting items like

Silver End Honey, Great Leighs Apple Juice and Canvey Island Cakes. Dotted around the shop you will find plastic recipe cards for you to help yourself. They give recipes for things like Creamy Parsnip Soup, Beefy Burgers, Rhubarb Crumble, Spinach and Sweet Potato Curry. I collected twelve cards and the good thing about them is that they won't spoil if they get splashed. I was very happy to find there was a recipe for Real Farmhouse Custard. Go on be adventurous, try it instead of opening a packet of Birds.

Before leaving the shop I noticed that it had a DIY livery stable attached, useful if you happen to have a horse. There is also a woodware shop selling things like bird tables and all sorts of wooden items. So when you've finished shopping, they could probably sell you a trug to put it all in.

I am addicted to mince, so I bought half a pound minced pork and half a pound minced lamb. At home I put them into separate bowls. I then peeled and grated two carrots and chopped up one large onion. I mixed them together and divided them into two. One I mixed into the lamb, adding a teaspoon of chopped mint and the other I mixed into the pork adding a teaspoon of chopped apple. I formed the mixtures into balls and deep fried them separately. Just an idea for you!

10

Buried within a modern industrial complex in Braintree, I found a company called Nature's Finest Foods, which surprised me. It is a small family business run by Mr Khurana and Mira; they produce nuts. I say produce but they don't actually make nuts; Mother Nature does that. They pack them for the wholesale market. Mr Khurana is an engineer by profession who came to this country and started the business in 1981. It seemed to me that this was a very courageous thing to do, for in England we have been buying and selling nuts for hundreds of years. However, along comes Mr Khurana and from very small beginnings, the company has grown enormously.

Fifty percent of the company's business is distributing their own Nature's Finest products and the other fifty percent is contract packing for other companies. They used to supply airlines with those little packets of nuts that you get with your first drink but this business has declined in recent years due to the scare of nut allergies. One of their most popular items was Bombay Mix but this has now been discontinued because they don't have sufficient staff to keep up with the demand. It was a labour intensive product and, since the opening of Stansted Airport, which poached a lot of staff in the district, they can no longer cope. In a week they produce six tons of oil-roasted nuts and three tons of air-roasted. All nuts are delivered within two days of roasting and all orders are delivered within a week.

Their range is wide and varied and I cannot give the complete list but it includes potato snacks, tortilla chips, Indian and Japanese style snacks and practically all the nuts known to man. Theirs is quite a success story. Although they do not sell retail, they would deliver an order to you provided it was for a minimum of £15, but there would be a delivery charge. Place your order online at orders@naturesfinest.co.uk

I made an unusual sandwich spread by combining some nuts with cream cheese. Grind any kind of nut you fancy, in a pestle and mortar until as fine as you can get them, then just mix into the cheese.

Leaving Braintree on the A131, follow the signs to Bocking and at Church Street you will find one of Essex's 18th century windmills. When it was built in 1721, it was out in the country, but now it is surrounded by houses. In the 1830s demand for housing was such that a great number of buildings surrounded the mill and it had to be moved to another location because it became shielded from the wind. A windmill without wind wasn't much good. History has subsequently repeated itself, because of a new development; it is now only open to the wind on one side.

Inside it is complete with all its gear and is presumably still in working order. However, it is only open to the public on a few occasions during the year because it is staffed by volunteers. If you do want to take a look inside, telephone 01376 3412339 to check first.

If you like wandering around beautiful, secluded and interesting gardens, go to Saling Hall. Take the B1256 out of Braintree and turn off at Blake End and Saling Hall is a little way up the road. Saling Hall is a 16th century Elizabethan manor house, which is not open to the public, but its twelve acre garden is. It is divided into several different gardens such as a Walled Garden, a Kitchen Garden, a Water Garden, a Japanese Garden and an arboretum. On a sunny day it is very pleasant, wandering around in peace and quiet, smelling the flowers and listening to the birds. You will be pleased to know that there is no gift shop, no plant sales and no café; all you get is the garden but really that's all you need.

It is open on Wednesdays only from 2pm to 5pm, May to July. Because it is not often open, it is remarkably quiet. When I was last there, I seemed to be the only visitor and that made it more intimate.

Make your way to the B1053 and, between Shalford and Wethersfield you will find Boydell's Dairy Farm. This working farm, which is open to the public, specialises in sheep's milk. There are lots of things to do here, hands on stuff like helping to milk a sheep. In the farm shop you can buy the sheep's cheeses, like Plumley and Lord of the Hundreds. Also on sale is sheep's ice cream, yoghurt and Yoggipops, sheep yoghurt ice lollies. What could be nicer; I'm told that they are.

Why not make a Sheep Sauce, using sheep's yoghurt? Take ¾ cup yoghurt, one cup grated sheep cheese, two tablespoons flour, one cup sheep's milk, half a teaspoon mustard powder, two tablespoons butter, salt and pepper. Mix the mustard powder with water. Melt the butter, add flour, cook for about a couple of minutes, add the milk slowly, stirring all the time, then add the yoghurt. Stir until absolutely smooth. Add the cheese, mustard, salt and pepper. Simmer until the cheese has melted. It goes well with any vegetable, on pasta, but especially with hard boiled eggs.

On your way north on the B184 you will come to Thaxted, which is the home of John Webbs Windmill. Built in 1804, it is probably in the best condition of any tower windmill in the country. It is, in fact, the only windmill left in Thaxted as, years ago there were several. It is no exaggeration to say that a lot of loving care and attention, as well as a lot of money, has been spent on restoration of this mill. Over the years it had fallen into disrepair several times, until finally in the 1970s the parish came to its rescue and with the help of local volunteers, it became a rural museum. Restoration work has been carried out several times since then. In 1996 it finally became a fully working mill. In 2010 disaster struck once again. One of the sales, called in the trade, 'sweeps' – I didn't know that – fell off and damaged the mill. Again public money was raised and the sweep replaced and the damage repaired. Now it could grind corn into flour if it wanted to but it doesn't, being simply a museum of country life.

It's normally open to the public in the afternoons of Saturday, Sunday and bank holidays from Easter to the end of September. Admission is free, but donations are welcome to help towards the cost of its upkeep. Do visit it, if only to say thank you to thousands of local people for saving this piece of Essex history.

From Thaxted carry on up the B184 to Saffron Walden, then follow the signs to Audley End. If however, you are approaching from London, just before the M11 launches you into Cambridgeshire, take the branch on to the A11, then slam the brakes on and turn on to the B1385 at junction 9A and follow that road till you get to Audley End, gleaming in the sunshine, beckoning you to come in. Audley End is the most beautiful house in Essex, probably the best in the country.

Built in about 1603 to impress and entertain King James I, it was at one time the largest private house in England, a palace in all but name. It is now only about one third of its original size, but still very large. There are plenty of things to see and do on the estate, in fact you can spend the whole day there. The restored Victorian Service Wing will give you a very good idea of how the servants of this grand house coped with the demands of the household and its many guests. No microwaves or dishwashers for them, everything had to be done by hand. The house was completely self-sufficient, everything, including fruit and vegetables, was produced on the estate. They kept their own animals for meat, shot their own birds for game and baked their own bread.

The house contains some beautiful interiors, furniture, rare tapestries and paintings by the likes of Holbein, Lely and Canaletto. I could go on, but it would only spoil it for you.

Give yourself and the family a treat and spend a day there, it will be a truly unforgettable experience.

Up in this north-western corner of Essex, is another of our iconic companies. It is up there with the big boys, Coles Traditional Foods Ltd. at Great Chesterford, just north of Saffron Walden. Mr Christopher Cole, the Managing Director who works out of his house a short distance from his factory, received me graciously and I enjoyed about an hour's conversation with him.

Perhaps the product that Coles is most known for is their Christmas pudding, undoubtedly the best in the land. I know them very well, for I used to buy them for Harvey Nichols when I was their food buyer and have eaten many since. Apart from the Christmas puddings, which come in many guises and packages, they also make good old Spotted Dick, Sticky Toffee, Rich Fruit and Whisky cake, Chocolate Fudge, Treacle Pudding and Orange Pudding. Even typing them out is making my mouth water. Fairly recent additions to their range are Brandy Butter and Mincemeat which completes the Christmas theme. Christopher gave me a flyer announcing another new product, so new at that time that it wasn't on the market. I'm sure it is now though. This was a pack of four Christmas puddings, made with Guinness, packed into a can. They looked so attractive, I know they will be a huge success.

Christopher's father, Mr Albert Cole, originally formed the company around 1939 and Chris took over in 1979. The original recipe for the Christmas pudding was created by Chris's great grandmother and the company known as A.J.Cole & Sons began making it in their original bakery as far back as 1939. The recipe remains unchanged to this day. Chris has added many other recipes since he took over. Apart from their own products, they create about 25/30 own label products for other companies and they supply all the high class outlets throughout the country and the world. All ingredients that are available in this country are sourced locally but some fruits have to come from overseas. The puddings are made one year in advance; so when you buy they are a year old and, like a good wine, the longer you keep them, the better they become. I always buy mine just before Christmas but it will not be eaten until the next Christmas, a year later. If you would like to buy, and I strongly recommend that you do, you can do so online at sales@colestrad.co.uk or by phone 01799 531053. Failing that, go to any high class grocer.

An educational day out for the kids is to be had at Mountfitchet Castle. Set just outside the ancient village of Stansted Mountfitchet, home of a famous working windmill, is the castle theme park. The 12th century castle was completely destroyed by King John – he of Magna Carta fame – and only a small fragment now remains. However, an historically accurate replica has now been built to educate and delight you. Inside the castle walls is a Norman village where you can enjoy the ambience of what life was like in medieval Essex. Friendly animals wander around the village and you can feed them, provided you buy a bag of feed from the farm shop – 50p.

Also in the complex is the House on the Hill Toy Museum. This is claimed to be the largest privately owned toy museum in Europe, housing some 800 toys from ancient times to the present day. You can enjoy what is called a Dinosaur Encounter and if they don't frighten you to death, try the Haunted Manor where the ghosts really exist. After that you can relax over a restorative cup of tea in the tea room, but be aware if you go into the gift shop, your children could cost you a lot of money.

The castle is open from March to November from 10am to 5pm. To get there, if you are coming from Great Chesterford direction, take the B1383 all the way to Stansted Mountfitchet or, if you are on the M11 leave at junction 8 and follow the tourist signs. Alternatively if you are on the A120, go around

Bishops Stortford and then pick up the tourist signs. Have a good day!

If you happen to be driving along the A120 intending to leave the county at Bishops Stortford, before you tumble into Hertfordshire, turn on to the B1256 and follow the signs to Hatfield Forest. This is one of the finest areas of forest in this country and Essex should be proud that it has preserved the only medieval forest there is. There are many forests in England but they have all been altered beyond recognition from what they once were. The New Forest is only a shadow of its former self and Sherwood Forest hardly exists at all any more. However, Hatfield Forest, laid out by King Henry II in the 12th century as his private hunting ground, still remains as the king left it. Nothing has altered.

It is open all year round and is free, but the National Trust ask you to pay a fee to park your car. Go and take a look and wander through an ancient area of natural beauty that hasn't changed for over 900 years. Lose yourself in the depths of the forest where you can almost hear the sound of the hunting horns of hundreds of years ago, and hear the whiz of medieval arrows as they ricochet off the ancient trees, some of which are 1200 years old and still standing. They were there long before old King Henry took over the forest. If only trees could talk. In fact, dendrologists say that they can but they are not too talkative to the likes of you and me.

Priors Hall Farm is a small country business of pure quality. Sitting deep in the Essex countryside just outside the village of Lindsell, it was so difficult to find that even the police were baffled.

On the outskirts of Great Dunmow, the famous flitch town, I pulled into a superstore car park to consult my map. As I did so, a police car pulled up alongside me and the driver asked if I needed help. I told him I was trying to find the village of Lindsell. Although he was a local lad, he did not know where Lindsell was. I told him that, according to my map, it was off the Finchingfield road but he insisted that it was off the Thaxted road. In spite of enquiring of the police station on his radio, we were none the wiser. In the end, he said he would lead me and I was to follow him. So, blue lights flashing, we sped off along the Thaxted road. After about five miles, travelling at 60 mph, I noticed the Priors Hall Farm sign on the right side of the road as we sped by. I flashed my lights at my leader who finally stopped a couple of miles further on. 'We've passed it, haven't we?' he said. With profuse apologies, he held up the traffic while I did a three point turn and bid me goodbye. So eventually I arrived at Priors Hall Farm.

It is a typical collection of farm buildings, one of which is labelled 'shop'. The two young men inside were not only serving, but butchering as well. It is a family business run by the Menhinick family, specialising in pork. Their pigs are fed with wheat and barley grown on their farm and this feed combined with the excellent conditions in which the animals are kept, makes the meat taste exceptionally good. In fact, customers say that Priors Hall pork tastes as pork used to.

Whilst they do sell chickens, free range eggs, some beef and lamb which come from local farms, their main product is pork. They have every type of pork you want, joints, chops, ribs, mince, sausages, burgers, bacon, and gammon. They will even sell you a 45 kilo hog roast, a suckling pig, or half a pig for your freezer. I was very impressed; Priors Hall Farm is a genuine Essex country farm to be proud of. By the way, if you do decide to buy from them, and I recommend you do, they accept credit cards.

I bought two pork hocks and this is what I did with them. In a large saucepan, I covered them with water and added a few whole black peppercorns. I stuck three or four cloves into a peeled onion. I cut an apple into four pieces, did not peel or core it and I took one carrot, left it whole, scrubbed it but did not peel it and with a bay leaf, put the lot into the saucepan, brought it to the boil and then let it simmer for an hour and a half. To go with it I cooked some spinach and when cooked, grated some nutmeg into it and served the hocks on it.

Another thing I like to do with pork is cook it in milk. Chop a couple of peeled carrots and two sticks of celery into pieces and sauté them with some garlic for about three minutes. Add a loin of pork, weighing about 1 ½ lb, brown it completely. Cover it with hot milk and cook slowly for two hours. Halfway through cooking, add the rind of half a lemon, some salt and freshly ground black pepper. About fifteen minutes before the end of cooking time, add two tablespoons of balsamic vinegar. By now the milk will have reduced and be thick. Serve it over slices of the meat.

From Great Dunmow, take the A130 until you see the sign for Barnston, then wind your way through the lanes to Bishops Green and here you will find one of my favourite farms and farm shops, Great Garnetts. When I was last there, I was met by Julie, joint owner with her husband, and very warmly welcomed. She told me about the origins of the company and explained what they did. We sat in the kitchen/canteen, which had been elevated to the status of boardroom while I was there. It is a family run concern and the whole gang seemed to be a very happy team, dedicated to their work. I was shown their herd of very contented sows and their charming, boisterous, happy piglets. I was also taken to where the sows lay whilst waiting to give birth, in what I believe are called 'arks'. I was then introduced to the butchery team, hard at work in the cutting room, where they cut the pork into joints, chops, etc. While I was there, they were making chipolata sausages and I found it fascinating watching the pork mix squeezing out of a nozzle directly into the natural sausage casing. It came out in one long line and was twisted into sausage lengths. It looked so easy but even though I was invited to try, I didn't dare. I was then shown the smokehouse where they make their bacon.

Great Garnetts make just three kinds of sausage, Old English, Cumberland and Traditional. This last is unique to them, having first been invented by a butcher in Saffron Walden. When the butcher shut up shop, the recipe was bought by Great Garnetts and I was very glad that they did, for this was the one I tried and it is probably the best sausage that I have ever eaten.

The farm shop is open Thursdays from 2pm to 5pm and Fridays from 9am to 1pm when the whole range is available. Also, Julie told me about the market they hold on the second Saturday of every month except January, August and September. Here you will find a huge range of the best locally produced food, including their own pork, as well as a whole selection of crafts. There are plenty of things to keep your children occupied while you are making your purchases and, by the way, every visitor gets a complimentary cup of tea or coffee.

The whole place had a very happy atmosphere, one of dedication to the best care of their pigs, ensuring them a happy, contented life, which in the end produces the very best meat. You really should make a visit as I certainly shall every time I'm in the area.

Before leaving, Julie gave me her recipe for Ginger Spiced Pork which she has very kindly allowed me to pass on to you. You will need one ounce of flour, one teaspoon of salt, freshly ground black pepper, one teaspoon ground ginger, 1 lb diced pork shoulder and one ounce of cooking oil. For the sauce, you need one teaspoon Tabasco sauce, two x 400g tins chopped tomatoes, eight ounces button mushrooms, two teaspoons Worcester sauce, four teaspoons vinegar, three chopped garlic cloves, and two bay leaves. Put all the sauce ingredients in a casserole dish. Mix all the dry ingredients together, coat the pork and fry it until well browned. Transfer to the casserole and mix with the sauce. Place in a pre-heated oven, gas mark 4, 350f, 180c for an hour. What more could you ask for?

Driving north on the A130 one sunny April day when, on a whim, I turned left to Onslow Green. I found myself on a small road running between dazzling green fields and very soon I came to a sign advertising Essex Larders. With a name like that I just had to investigate. I turned into the entrance and found myself in the charming Pyes Farm courtyard. Pretty, well kept houses lined three sides of a square and the whole place exuded peace and tranquility. Little did I think that beneath this calm exterior there lurked a thriving business. But it certainly did.

This was the home of Essex Larders, a one time fruit farm turned bakery. Jane, the owner, showed me around and introduced me to her products. They make probably the most exciting range of pies and puddings that you will ever come across. Such pies as Venison and Blackcurrant, Gammon and Cranberry, Duck and Sage. They also make the famous Dunmow Flitch Pasty as well as several quiches including Lorraine. Apple pies are also in their range, so is Sticky Toffee Pudding. Jane showed me a raised pie, straight out of the oven that made my mouth water just to look at it.

Unfortunately Essex Larders do not sell retail, so don't try to go there. But it would be well worth you looking for their products in such places as farm shops throughout Essex and at Delicious Deli in Dunmow, Bakers Deli in Felsted, Sceptred Isle in Saffron Walden, Budgens in Ingatestone and Calcott Hall, Brentwood. Many local pubs and restaurants have them on their menus but if you live in the capital, you should go to Harrods, Fortnum & Mason or Partridges. For such quality, where else?

On my way to Chelmsford on the A130 I stopped in Little Waltham and found Sonia Clere. Tonia, the owner, runs a small business of outside caterers and has been doing so for over twenty years. If you are giving a party or a banquet, place an order with Tonia, tell her exactly what you want and she will cater to you to your heart's content. Download her information at www.soniaclere.co.uk and you will see the sort of cakes she can produce. The site also gives you a list of the sort of events they cater for. You need to order by phone at 01245 363990 or online and Sonia Clere will deliver to you. You cannot collect from them, that is probably why the company was a bit shy giving me their address. All I can tell you is that it is in Little Waltham.

11

Approaching the western border of Essex, just before it becomes Hertfordshire at Bishops Stortford, you will come to the village of Hatfield Broad Oak. As ever in searching out remote addresses, it can be like looking for a needle in a haystack. Parts of Essex are very remote, signposts rare and street names non-existent. My map tells me to turn right at Church Lane; there is a lane on my right but it is keeping its name secret. So what does one do, take a chance? Well if you do, you could end up back in Chelmsford! In the present case I was looking for Hatfield Broad Oak but that wasn't the village I needed, for my address said Cage End. After wandering around for a while I finally spotted a Cage End signpost, which was covered in the verdigris of a hundred years. I followed this lane into another tiny village which seemed most unlikely to be the home of a large factory making sausages. I enquired of a gentleman walking his dog. He told me to turn left at the village hall, which I did and found myself in what looked like the grounds of a grand house. The area was called Newbury Meadow, which didn't appear in my address. However, surrounded by carefully mown lawns, immaculate flower beds and stately trees, was the very modern Broad Oak Sausage factory. I parked the car but was immediately cautioned by a man standing by the door not to leave it there as they had large articulated lorries coming in and out all day and my car could get damaged. I had difficulty in believing that juggernauts could negotiate the narrow lanes of Cage End Village, but who knows?

Upstairs in the office, I was led into the boardroom by the second generation owner, Mr Roger Simmons. He began by telling me the history of the company, of which he was justly proud. The company was founded in 1927 by the village doctor, Dr White. Apparently he ran the business as a sideline, for he was a farmer as well as the village doctor. Roger's father was the village butcher who bought his meat from Dr White. When the good doctor retired, Mr Simmons Senior bought the business and Roger began working for his dad.

The original sausage recipe came from Roger's grandmother in Ireland and it is still one of their best sellers. They had to borrow £150 from the bank in order to pay for their first week's meat. The business was steady until the 1940s when it began to suffer from wartime restrictions. In 1966 the company was producing 5cwt of sausages a week; now they turn out twenty tons.

Although this is still a family business, it is no longer a small country business; it is up there with the big boys, one of Essex's top companies. Of course they don't sell retail, but should you go to Tesco, Asda and Morrisons and you will find the Broad Oak Label. Their sausages are also in Budgens and Londis under the retailers' labels. You can also find them at farmers' markets and country fairs throughout East Anglia.

Roger insisted that I took some sausages away with me, a generous gesture, one that shows how proud he is of his product, rightly so in my opinion. Bangers and mash seemed too ordinary for these wonderful sausages, so I grilled, not fried, six sausages, then cut them in half lengthways. I then made up a thick beef gravy, added a generous amount of chilli powder and flooded the sausages with it. A real hot dog!

In Chelmsford there is another of Essex's famous companies. This time a flour miller, W & H Marriage & Sons Ltd. For the past 100 years, Marriages have been milling flour in Chelmsford and, five generations later, they are still doing it. They produce a wide range of flours; flours for every conceivable purpose. Not only that, they also produce animal feeds. Their wheat is locally grown and milled right here. A bi-product of the milling, the residue, goes into their animal feeds. This is sold to practically every farmer in the district and many local farm shops too. They are very much an Essex born company, probably one of the most famous in the county.

The mill is not open to the public, but you can buy Marriage's flour everywhere in Essex. From what I have seen, I would say that it is stocked in every farm shop and local grocery store in the county. In the course of a conversation with Mr George Marriage, he gave me permission to pass on to you one of their interesting recipes; it is for Sticky Sweet Malted Loaf.

You will need :

450G Marriage's Organic Country Fayre Malted Brown flour.

6 tablespoons malt extract

3 tablespoons golden syrup

50g dark brown muscovado sugar

300 ml milk

A good pinch of salt

2 teaspoons baking powder

50g unsalted butter, diced

100 g sultanas

2 large free range eggs, beaten to mix.

Here's what you do:

Heat your oven to 160C, 325F or gas 3. Weigh out the malt, golden syrup, sugar and milk and place together in a small pan; heat gently, stirring constantly until smooth. Remove from the heat and leave to cool. Combine the flour with the salt in a mixing bowl. Add the diced butter and rub in with your fingers until the mixture looks like fine crumbs. With a wooden spoon, mix in the sultanas followed by the milk mixture, together with the eggs to make a smooth, thick batter. Pour into prepared tins and spread evenly. Bake in the oven for about an hour or until a skewer inserted into the centre comes out clean. Towards the end of cooking time, stir two tablespoons of boiling hot milk and one tablespoon of caster sugar, to make a thin, runny sticky glaze. As soon as the loaves come out of the oven, brush this glaze over them. Then set on a cooling rack and leave until completely cold before turning out. This will make two medium loaves and you will need 2 x 450g/1lb loaf tins, greased and lined with a strip of greaseproof paper to cover the base and sides.

While I was in Chelmsford I found, tucked away in a little modern housing development very close to the centre of town, The Chocolate Truffle Co. run by Christine Moss. For the last three years she has been making eleven different varieties of chocolate truffle. She told me that the most popular one was Champagne, but I suppose if you ate a whole boxful of them, you wouldn't get drunk. She also makes chocolate bars, lollipops and little chocolate figures. You could order from her by telephone on 01245 257628 or online at www.thechocolatetrufflecompany and she will post them to you. Alternatively you will find her at the Great Garnetts market on the second Saturday of every month or the range is usually on display in Ashlyns farm shop, Ongar.

I haven't tried Christine's truffles yet, but when I do I shall carry out a small experiment. I shall take a few of her flavoured truffles, and gently melt them down in a small saucepan over boiling water to see if I can turn them into an interesting sauce. Why don't you have a go?

When in Chelmsford, why not visit one of this country's smallest cathedrals? It might well be the smallest in the country but it serves one of the largest dioceses. It is also the parish church of the county town. To underline its importance, the church of St Mary was also dedicated to two other saints, St Peter and St Cedd. A church was originally built on this site in about 1200 but many alterations and restorations have taken place since then. In 1914 it became a cathedral when the first bishop was enthroned. Then in 1983 it was extensively refurbished and the bishop's chair, known as a Cathedra, was installed. From the outside it looks too small to be a cathedral but once inside, you will be surprised to find how big it really is.

If you love browsing in antique shops or are looking for a particular something, visit Baddow Antique Centre situated in the middle of the village of Great Baddow. There are thirty traders displaying their wares, including furniture, paintings, grandfather clocks, silver, porcelain and glass. They are open seven days a week from 10am to 5pm. I found what I was looking for when I was there, and you might too.

On my way out of Chelmsford, I passed through Galleywood where Lathcoats Farm Shop is situated and it needs no introduction from me. It is possibly one of the most popular farm shops in Essex. People come from all over the county to shop there and indeed, each time I've been there, it has been busy. There is always a queue at the cash tills.

It is more than a farm shop, it is a working farm where you can say hello to the pigs, goats and donkeys, pick your own berries – even boysenberries – in season. If you wish, you can rent a tree and all the apples it produces are yours and yours alone. In the shop, apart from their own fruit, you will find an abundance of Galleywood grown vegetables, including asparagus. Locally laid, free range eggs are there aplenty. Lathcoats search the county for products to sell from small, specialist producers. It might be said that they have some of the finest products that Essex provides. This is why there will always be a lot to tempt you.

In the shop, the courgettes looked green and shiny, so I bought some. I grated them on a coarse grater, and then chopped up a small onion very fine. I sautéed them together in a little vegetable oil. I crushed up some dried Marjoram and sprinkled it on the courgettes while they were cooking. Takes about three minutes.

I also boiled some of Lathcoats' potatoes and instead of mashing them, I crushed them roughly. I sautéed a finely minced onion lightly in butter and mixed it into the potato. On another occasion I mashed up some potato with butter and milk, then took a young carrot, didn't peel it, but you can if it doesn't look young enough, then lightly shaved it with a potato peeler and mixed the flakes into the mash. It tasted good and looked very pretty on the plate.

Squeezed between the A12 and the A130, snuggling up cosily alongside the Hanningfield Reservoir you will find West Hanningfield. Finding Blind Lane was more by luck than satnav. However, find it I eventually did. If you are better at following satnav directions than I am and get to New Barn Farm in Blind Lane, you will find it well worth the effort.

Leaning on the farm gate, I found the farmer, Trevor Robb, talking with a neighbour. I was greeted in a most jocular manner and he suggested I talk to his wife, Pauline. She was exceedingly friendly and was only too pleased to show me around the farm. She was dressed for the occasion in farming clothes including wellies and I regretted that I wasn't as well. We trudged through muddy ground to inspect the free range chickens and ducks. I was introduced to Squeak, their prize boar and Dossie, his sow. He was a friendly beast and I congratulated him when I discovered that he had two more sows at his command. It is most unusual for farmers to name their animals, but Pauline assured me that all their animals have names. Between the three sows, Squeak manages to produce up to sixty piglets a year. Some are sold on at about eight weeks old, but there was only one cute little piglet left when I was there. The pigs destined for the butchers are kept for up to six months.

As well as pork, they also produce beef. They have twenty-nine cows, mainly Dexters but including two Herefords plus a bull who, Pauline assured me, was very friendly. I decided nevertheless, not to put him to the test. They produce packs of their beef ready for the freezer from 12 to 15 kilos; too big for me.

Their poultry, ducks and chickens wander freely around their twenty acres, laying their eggs which are sold on. Pauline buys chicks but not ducklings. The ducks on the farm are immigrants, having all been donated. People who keep ducks often decide, for one reason or another, to get rid of them. They bring them to New Barn Farm where Trevor and Pauline are more than happy to give them a home. So if you have a bird that you are tired of feeding, head for Blind Lane.

Pauline is a sympathetic, caring farmer but a little unusual. She describes herself as a farming banker. Her day job is with a German bank in the City of London. She often spends four days a week in Munich, one day in London and two days at home on the farm. An interesting lifestyle; a most unusual farmer. If you would like to get in touch with her, go online www.newbarnfarm.co.uk and see what comes up.

Whenever I am seduced into buying a joint of pork from a supermarket, I am invariably disappointed in the crackling; I wonder if you feel the same. If I got my hands on one of Pauline's pork joints, I'm sure I'd have better luck. The secret is, I am told, make sure the skin is dry with salt well rubbed in. Sea salt is best. Put it in a very hot oven for about twenty minutes, then turn the heat down to the normal roasting temperature for the rest of the cooking time. Bon appetit!

Before leaving Chelmsford completely, take a look at Hylands House. It's on the main London road, the A414 just south of the town. Originally built in 1730 as a Queen Anne style red brick house, it has had several makeovers since then. It wasn't until 1814 that the house was remodelled into the classic style we see today.

It has had several owners and a somewhat chequered career. In World War One it became a hospital and in World War Two, a prisoner of war camp. Not many allied prisoners of war were housed in such elegant surroundings, for although Colditz was a castle, it was a pretty grim looking one. In 1944 the SAS set up their headquarters in the house and it was then that an army captain tried to drive his Jeep up the grand staircase. The driver was packed off to bed to 'sleep it off' and the Jeep had to be dismantled in order for it to be removed.

The house was finally purchased by Chelmsford Borough Council in 1966 and they have been slowly carrying out a complete restoration since then. It is now back to its original Georgian condition. You can wander through the Georgian elegance of the dining room and the exquisitely gilded neo-baroque banqueting room. The drawing room has been restored to its Victorian splendour and the whole house exudes wealth and opulence. You can hire the place for a conference or a banquet and you can even get married there. In the restored stable block, various events and workshops are held and once a month, there is a farmers' market. Chelmsford Council has done an excellent job and the house now deserves to be appreciated.

In the village of Ingatestone, a few miles south of Chelmsford, right in the middle of the high street, is Ravens of Ingatestone, the bakers. It is probably one of the best known bakers in the county. Giselle Hyland runs the only award-winning bakery in Essex. She makes and bakes everything that is sold in the shop. From individual cakes and pastries, gateaux, buns, right up to every kind of bread. She also does a wonderful range of the presently fashionable cupcakes. These diminutive cupcakes, so called because they are baked in small cups, originated in the United States in the 19th century. I remember as a child, we called them fairy cakes. Now they are baked in greaseproof paper cups and can be served in them, especially if they are creamy, when they protect your fingers. But, you know one of the best things about eating creamy, sticky cupcakes is that you can lick your fingers afterwards.

If you are planning a birthday, a christening or a wedding, Giselle will design and make a speciality cake for you. From the sample book I was shown, they are absolutely stunning. If they taste half as good as they look, they will be marvellous. It was Halloween time when I was there and the shop was surrounded by gingerbread skeletons. Another of her specialities at Christmas is gingerbread men, which I suppose might be the Halloween skeletons with flesh on their bones. If you want something different to decorate your Christmas tree, try Giselle's Father Christmas figures, because you can eat them afterwards, if you're not too full.

There are a few tables and chairs in the shop where you can rest and enjoy a cup of tea or coffee and a cake, bun or sausage roll. I did and I can recommend it.

After leaving Ravens of Ingatestone, carry on up the High Street until you come to the sign for Ingatestone Hall. This 16th century manor house remains almost entirely as it was built in Tudor days. Most stately homes have changed over the centuries, each successive occupant putting their imprint on them. Bringing them up to date, modernising, so that a house built in the 16th century is modified in the 17th, brought up to date in the 18th, modernised in the 19th and often gets ruined in the 20th century. This is not so with Ingatestone Hall. The secret is that, having been built by Sir William Petre, the Petre family still occupy the house. The house is open to the public on Wednesdays, Sundays and Bank Holiday Mondays, from 12 noon to 5.00pm. Although the house hasn't changed, the orchards that once surrounded it have disappeared but the gardens do still retain a Tudor feel.

Inside, you will find the Summer Parlour – probably too cold to use in the winter – the original ballroom, which is available for private dinners and receptions. The Stone Hall is lined with some wonderful oak panelling, the Old Kitchen, with its cavernous open fireplace, is impressive and My Master's Lodging still contains its original four poster bed. The forty metre long Gallery, created to provide the occupants of the house with an exercise area on wet days, has a display of family portraits and memorabilia accumulated over the centuries. Finally, the house boasts two priests' holes concealed within the thickness of the walls. Being a catholic family, they looked after their priests. They'll look after you too, for you can take a guided tour; give it a try.

Nearby Ingatestone is Spring Farm the home of A.B.Roots. It is tucked away just outside the village of Fryerning and was surprisingly easy to find. Turn into the Fryerning Lane off Ingatestone High Street, you will soon come to Blackmore Road and Spring Farm is well signposted from there.

Now this is really a typical small Essex farm business, run it would seem, solely by Yvonne Roots, sometimes assisted by her young daughter but who wants to be a dancer, not a farmer. I don't know which profession is more precarious! She works from a small shed in the farmyard, which is surrounded by old machinery and an old car or two. In fact it reminded me of the farmyard depicted in the series *The Darling Buds of May*; it certainly had the same welcoming feel.

Yvonne produces eggs, only eggs, organic eggs from her Black Rock hens. Her hens, hundreds of them, all jet black, wander at will in the fields around the farm. It beats me how she can collect the eggs, with the hens spread out over seventeen acres, but apparently the hens retire to nest boxes to lay. And who said chickens were not intelligent? I have to say that it was a delightful, rural sight seeing the hens, like black dots spreading away into the distance, doing what hens ought to do, enjoying themselves, pecking up food and grit.

Whilst they do have a happy, natural life, Yvonne did admit that they have a problem with foxes. A fox is partial to a chicken, and several are taken every week. She is somewhat philosophical about it, saying that with 2000 hens at any one time, it is not too much of a problem. She buys her chicks locally when they are one day old, rears them and sells their eggs. She will sell retail from the farm, but the majority are sold wholesale, one of her best customers being Budgens. She sells by the half dozen and in large trays to local shops all over

Essex and especially to a farm shop in Brentwood. She gave me half a dozen, one of which I boiled the next day for breakfast. I don't know if it was my imagination, but I did think it tasted much better than the ones I buy in Tescos.

The versatile egg, can be boiled, fried, poached, scrambled and coddled, of course, but you can make some changes. Instead of soft boiling, you can hard boil it, take off the shell and put it into a square egg press, leave it a couple of minutes and, hey presto, you have a perfectly square egg. You can, I believe get a square egg press on eBay. If you have a child in the house, paint a face on an egg, soft boil it, but make sure the colour is waterproof. If you fry an egg, get a metal cookie cutter, such as a star, a heart or a simple crinkly one; grease it well, crack an egg into it and you'll end up with a lovely shaped fried egg. A delight for the kids. When poaching, don't put vinegar in the water. Fill a small frying pan with water, bring it to the boil, turn it down to a simmer, stir the water with a wooden spoon so that it is swirling round, carefully break your egg into it, when it will poach beautifully. You can add anything you like into scrambled egg, especially smoked salmon. For a coddled egg, add a little grated cheese and a teaspoon of cream and coddle away.

For a quick, easy meal, boil some new potatoes; when done, cut them into pieces. Sauté a chopped onion till translucent, add the potatoes, a chopped, seeded red pepper, a few button mushrooms, quartered and a few asparagus tips. Finally add a chopped garlic and cook on for a few minutes. Add some beaten eggs, as many as you need, and cook on until the eggs are set. Simply delicious and highly nutritious.

Carry on down to Brentwood to Old MacDonald's Farm for a fun day out for the kids. It has exactly what it says in the old song. There are lots of things for children to play with and animals galore. Ponies, reindeer, goats, pigs, cows, rabbits, tortoises, otters, meerkats, chickens and even rhea. What's a rhea, I hear you ask. It is a bird from South America, a bit like a miniature ostrich, quite rare in this county. It is a flightless bird, so how it got to Brentwood, I don't know. Perhaps it swam! Anyway, what I have mentioned is only half the fun at Old MacDonald's Farm. Why not visit and let your child be the judge.

On Ongar Road, Brentwood, you will find Calcott Hall Farm; it crouches right beside the A12 Brentwood bypass. It's an Aladdin's cave of fresh local produce. The list of things they grow is endless, but don't expect fruit or vegetables out of season. In season, while I was there, was rhubarb and very fresh and clean it looked. About a couple of weeks after my visit, they were expecting their first crop of asparagus and I'm sure you'll not find better anywhere.

The shop was very busy but in spite of this, the manager took time out from his cash register to show me around. Not everything in the shop is produced on site, but their beef, lamb and chicken is all local. Their fruits include strawberries and raspberries but their vegetables include potatoes, cabbage, broccoli, cauliflower, carrots, beetroots, leeks, squash, peas, broad beans, onions, lettuce and even celeriac. No wonder those cash tills keep ringing. The shop was beautifully laid out and the displays so attractive it really did make me want to buy. And it will you too; give it a try.

While I was there, the manager gave me the Calcott Hall recipe for Loin of pork with rhubarb sauce. He has very kindly allowed me to pass it on to you. You will need, four strips of lemon zest, l.75kilo pork loin, skin removed. two garlic cloves, sliced, one tablespoon chopped, fresh parsley, salt, 20ml vegetable oil, 300 ml dry white wine. For the rhubarb sauce, you will need: 400g rhubarb cut into 5cm batons, 200g caster sugar, 300ml white wine. This is what you do.

Preheat the oven to 190c/375f/gas5/160c fan assist.

Bring a small saucepan of water to the boil, add the lemon zest and blanch for one minute. Drain and refresh under cold running water, then finely slice the zest with a sharp knife.

With a small pointed knife, make several incisions in the pork. Into each incision poke a little shredded lemon zest, garlic and parsley, then season with salt. Heat the oil in a roasting pan and, when it is smoking hot, lay the pork in the pan fat side down. While cooking turn it occasionally to brown evenly, then transfer to the hot oven to roast for thirty minutes. Remove the pan from the oven and tip out any fat. Pour in the wine and continue roasting for forty minutes.

Meanwhile, for the rhubarb sauce, place the rhubarb, sugar and wine into a saucepan and cook gently until the rhubarb is softened. To serve, place a little of the rhubarb sauce onto each plate. Slice the pork and place it on the plate just off centre.

Just south of Brentwood at Little Warley is the Brentwood Park Ski & Snowboard Centre. There are plenty of signs to the ski centre, so once you get to Warley, you won't get lost. Here you can have a lot of fun. Ski lessons and, what is more important, Snowboard Courses. Snowboarding has become very popular recently and is competing with skiing. However, it is not as easy as it looks and you should get yourself proficient before you head off into the Alps on holiday. This is most important for the children because snowboarding is very popular among them and, if it is not done properly, it can be dangerous.

If you happen to find yourself driving on the A12 and have time to spare, especially if you have kids in the car, turn off for Billericay and follow the brown tourist signs to Barleylands.

Barleylands is the home of the Essex Country Show, which is held in September. The rest of the year it is a country leisure park with lots of things to do, especially for the children and is an excellent day out. For the adults, there is plenty of retail therapy to indulge in. You can find glasswork, pottery, clothing and textiles to name but a few temptations.

There is even a working blacksmith on site, so if you have your horse with you, he can get shod while you wander about. You can buy fresh local produce too at the Barleylands Farmers' Market and you can dine in style in the Magic Mushroom restaurant, but when I was there, Magic Mushrooms were not on the menu. For a lighter meal, go to The Hive, where you will not get stung. Barleylands is certainly well worth a visit.

12

Take the A414 out of Chelmsford and in the area of North Weald you will come to Ashlyns Farm Shop which is perhaps the most important organic food suppliers in Essex. They grow wheat, barley, oats and rye and they sell their own and many other producers' products, almost entirely organic. A few of the unusual names that caught my eye were Highgrove Fish Stock, Handy Crabmeat, Meah's, Simply Delicious, Crazy Jack and much, much more. They organise farm visits, especially for schools, and they have a training kitchen to help dinner ladies produce healthy meals for the children. In the summer, on Fridays, they have a barbecue and they also hold season parties, like a Pumpkin Party at Halloween and many more. If you are of an organic frame of mind, you will find Ashlyns a treasure trove. You will discover all the organic produce that you could possibly want. It is not possible to list everything they sell, so why not go there and find out for yourself.

Their organic range of dried herbs is extensive and from the range I suggest you could make a creamy, tarragon sauce. You will need ¼ cup butter, one tablespoon flour, one cup milk, half a cup sour cream. One teaspoon each of dried tarragon, chervil, basil, and garlic powder. Half a teaspoon each of salt and freshly ground black pepper.

Melt the butter in a saucepan, stir in the flour, cook for a couple of minutes. Gradually add the milk. Cook stirring all the time until thickened. Take off the heat and stir in the sour cream and the dried herbs. Mix very well. When ready to serve, heat it up gently and serve with chicken or fish.

Drive west on the A414 and, before falling into the snares of Hertfordshire, turn left on to the B181, pass Roydon station, through the High Street and turn left into Harlow Road. There you will find East End Farm. Mrs Abbey who runs the farm, will serve you in her farm shop during October and November with her specially reared turkeys and chickens for Christmas. She also has free range eggs and other local produce.

This farm, which mainly grows arable crops for the wholesale trade, has been in existence for over fifty years, so they ought to know what they are doing. They never advertise, do not appear at any farmers' markets and their birds are only available direct from them. You can telephone an order on 01279 793125 or by e-mail at eastendfarm@btconnect.com or, if you wish to visit their web page go to www.turkeyshere.co.uk

To make a chicken taste that little bit better, what I do is mash up a chicken stock cube into some butter. Loosen the skin from the breast and, with your fingers push as much butter mix under the skin as far as you can. Fix the skin back with a cocktail stick or skewer. Put a bunch of fresh tarragon inside the cavity, or if you can't find fresh, use dried. In this case mix dried tarragon with sea salt and black pepper and sprinkle it into the cavity. Roast in the usual way and serve with a creamy tarragon sauce.

Now you must turn round, lest you fall out of our county. Make for Muskham Road in Harlow. Here there is the Museum of Harlow which has a wonderful collection of objects, text and pictures telling the story of the area from ancient times to the present day. Entrance to the museum is free and they are open from Tuesday to Saturday from 10am to 5pm.

While you are in Harlow and you feel like a rest, you could go to a beautiful example of a typical English garden, which is situated in Marsh Lane off the B183 Gilden Way in

Old Harlow, The Gibberd Garden. It was opened to the public after the death of the owner, Sir Frederick Gibberd, a landscape designer. In his will he stipulated that his garden should be available to the people of Harlow to enjoy for their recreation and education. The garden consists of glades, groves, pools and alleys providing settings for some 890 sculptures, architectural salvage, large ceramic pots, a gazebo and even a children's moated castle. Sounds fun, why not give it a try?

In the area around nearby Ongar, there are several places of interest to visit. One is the North Weald Airfield, an old Battle of Britain airfield of World War Two. Flying still takes place there as well as many sporting activities. It is also the home of one of the biggest open air markets, held every Saturday.

Another place to visit would be the Epping and Ongar Railway, in Ongar High Street. However, at the time of writing the railway was closed for re-development, but it is now fully open. The track of this historic railway runs through some beautiful Essex countryside and a ride in one of the old coaches would be a great experience for trainspotting types. For up to date information go to their web page on www.eorailway.co.uk or, if you fancy giving a helping hand, telephone them on 01277 365200.

Also nearby is the church of St Andrew in the village of Greensted-Juxta-Ongar; a curious name but I can tell you that 'Juxta' merely means near. It's a long name for a very tiny village. The church was originally thought to have been built in the 9th century, but more recent date tests have concluded that it was built in the 11th century. However, it is still one of the oldest wooden buildings still standing in the world. It was built of logs cut from Epping Forest and those of the north and west walls still remain. A curious thing is the 'leper's squint': a hole cut in the wooden wall so that lepers, who were forbidden to enter the church, could be blessed by the priest.

The church now has a tower, which was added in the 17th century. It is situated in a leafy part of the village at the end of a narrow lane and services are still held there every Sunday. It was a sunny day when I was there and it presented a truly magical atmosphere.

Retrace your steps out of the village to the A128, turn right for Kelvedon Hatch and you will come to another of Essex's curiosities. The Secret Nuclear Bunker. So secret in fact that there are signs to it all over the area! This is very much part of the history of the 20th century. At the end of the Second World War, it was dug out by the government on requisitioned farmland to provide offices and accommodation for ministers, probably including the Prime Minister and 600 military and civilian personnel. It was to be used in the event of a nuclear attack, to control and organise the aftermath of a nuclear explosion and to provide a safe area for the continued functioning of the government. At the end of the cold war, it was considered redundant and the original owner of the land bought it back and it has now become a tourist attraction. The area not only includes the bunker but it has an adventure park containing the only Rope Runners course in Essex, where you can walk the ropes from tree to tree in the woods. Also there is what is called a Tunnel Adventure, where you can grope about in the dark – great fun! – and you can even go Water Zorbing, whatever that is. Sounds far too energetic for me but your children will love it.

Do pigs giggle? Well Essex girl Tracy Mackness thinks they do. I tracked her down in the wilds of Romford. The town is not known exactly for its wild, unspoilt countryside, but on Saturday nights it could be wild in another sense. Founded in medieval times, it was once an important Essex market town. Things changed in the sixties, when it became a London borough, however, there is still one farm there.

At 132 Petersfield Avenue, Harold Hill you will find the Giggly Pig Company. In 2007, just after being released from prison, Tracy put her energies to good use and founded the company. From very small beginnings, breeding pigs, a skill she learned while in prison, she started making a few sausages. In three years she has developed from making just a very few sausages into a company manufacturing sixty-five different varieties. She now supplies pork joints from her Saddleback pigs and produces her own bacon. She says she has up to 300 pigs running around Romford at any one time but you won't see many of them in the High Street. She also does outside catering for parties, barbecues, weddings, etc. supplying Hog Roasts.

Giggly Pig sausages include varieties such as Caribbean, Spicy Romany, Welsh Dragon (I assume this has leek in it), and Wow, a sausage to be handled with care, unless you like it hot. I haven't tried them all – I don't think anyone has – but those that I have tried are very good. But one of my favourites has to be the Faggots. These may well hark back to the medieval days, being a very ancient dish that is largely forgotten these days, but they are really excellent.

This company is a true success story, for in three short years it has gone from a one woman band to a concern employing twelve people producing sixty-five different varieties of sausage and trading at over twenty-one farmers' markets in London and the South East. So if there isn't a farmers' market near you, hot foot it to their shop in Petersfield Avenue, Romford and you will not be disappointed.

It isn't the pigs that should be giggling, it should be Tracy Mackness herself and she has a lot to giggle about.

I have married up twenty-two varieties of sausage with some suggestions; see what you think.

Bramley Apple – Apple Sauce and Mixed Spice
Cracked Black Pepper – Mashed Potatoes and Chives
Discworld Ale – Fried Onions
Ginger and Spring Onion – Wild Rocket
Pork and Jalapeno – Red Pepper Puree
Stilton and Apple – Bread Sauce

Caribbean – Buttered Noodles
Classy Pork – Baked Beans
Old English – Chips
Spicy Garlic – Mashed Potatoes
The Irish – Shredded Cabbage
Pork and Leek – Cream Cheese
Hickory Smoked – Peanut Butter
Honey and Mustard – Mushy Peas
Highlander Banger – Thick Beef Gravy
Pork and Chestnut – Cranberry Sauce
Spicy Cumberland – Spinach
Sweet Lime and Chilli – Tomato Sauce
Hop Sausages – Glass of Beer
Stilton and Celery – Green Salad
Welsh Dragon – Cheesy Leeks
Wow wow – Rice

To round up our tour of Essex, in this south-western corner of the county, cheek by jowl to London, there are several places of interest for a good day out. For instance in Upminster is the Tithe Barn which contains the Museum of Nostalgia in Hall Lane. It is housed in the so-called Tithe Barn but there is no evidence that it ever collected tithes. Built in 1450 by the Abbot of Waltham Abbey, it is a fascinating building that contains an incredible collection of oldy-worldy things. Give it a try; at least you will be out of the rain.

In 1914 a place was needed where the new-fangled flying machines could take off and land. The government chose Hornchurch. RAF Hornchurch was developed to cope with the second world war and it played an important part in the Battle of Britain. Now that the Spitfires and Hurricanes have gone and the Royal Air Force has departed, the airfield has been turned into the Hornchurch Country Park.

Remnants of the airfield remain but that is not the real reason for visiting the park. The real reason is to view the habitat of a great variety of wildlife, the extensive tree plantations, the grassland, marshes, ponds, a lake and a river. Now it's a tranquil place where the wildlife can enjoy peace, no longer disturbed by the roar of aircraft engines. You can enjoy it too but if you insist of revisiting the past, you can explore the remains of what was once RAF Hornchurch to your heart's content.

If you are in the mood for a stroll or a longer walk in real country that is not too far from London, you could do no better than Belhus Woods Country Park. The Estate was once privately owned but now it belongs to Essex County Council. The whole park is managed by rangers, including the newly planted woodland, which is partly owned by the Forestry Commission and the Woodland Trust. Both organisations are dedicated to the preservation of wildlife and woodland.

Traditional coppicing is still carried out on the estate and this provides products for traditional crafts, including thatching and hurdle making. In the Spring, the woodland floor is a carpet of Bluebells of such density that it will take your breath away. Spring is also a good time to hear songbirds and to feed the ducks, grebes and geese. Also on the estate is a model railway, a boat club and an archery field, where you can be Robin Hood for a day.

The park is open all the year round, except for 25th December, from 8.00am to dusk and the visitor centre from 10.00am to 4.00pm. Oh and by the way, unlike many country parks, you can take your dog with you to this one, but do please keep him under control.

An absolute must to visit is Rainham Hall, a fine 18th century mansion right in the middle of the town on The Broadway. It was built in the Dutch style, which was popular in the early 1700s, by a Captain John Harle to show off the excellent building materials his company sold. We know that housing developers build show houses, well Rainham Hall is a show house par excellence.

Before finally ending our tour of Essex, why not try the Rainham Marshes Nature Reserve on New Tank Hill Road,

Purfleet. The area of the marshes was strictly reserved for the military, for training and exercises. Members of the public were forbidden. However, in 2000 the Royal Society for the Protection of Birds took a lease on the area and have turned it into a wonderful nature reserve. It is well signposted in the area and when you get there, you will not be disappointed. The marshes are an unspoilt landscape that provides a safe haven for many hundreds of bird species, wild animals and insects. You will be surprised at the variety you can see. Don't forget to take your camera with you but sorry, you can't take your doggie.

I have only just scraped surface of Essex. There are lots more things to do and see, places to visit and farm shops to buy from in the county. I only hope that this book has whetted your appetite and you will agree with me that there is a lot more to Essex than meets the eye.

Index

Recipe Index